Social Media for Creative Libraries

Social Media for Creative Libraries

Second edition of
How to Use Web 2.0 in Your Library

Phil Bradley

facet publishing

© Phil Bradley 2007, 2015

Published by Facet Publishing
7 Ridgmount Street, London WC1E 7AE
www.facetpublishing.co.uk

Facet Publishing is wholly owned by CILIP: the Chartered Institute of
Library and Information Professionals.

Phil Bradley has asserted his right under the Copyright, Designs and
Patents Act 1988 to be identified as author of this work.

Except as otherwise permitted under the Copyright, Designs and
Patents Act 1988 this publication may only be reproduced, stored or
transmitted in any form or by any means, with the prior permission of
the publisher, or, in the case of reprographic reproduction, in
accordance with the terms of a licence issued by The Copyright
Licensing Agency. Enquiries concerning reproduction outside those
terms should be sent to Facet Publishing, 7 Ridgmount Street, London
WC1E 7AE.

British Library Cataloguing in Publication Data
A catalogue record for this book is available from the British Library.

ISBN 978-1-85604-713-5

First published 2007 as *How to Use Web 2.0 in Your Library*
This second edition 2015

Text printed on FSC accredited material.

Typeset from author's files in 10/14 pt Palatino Linotype and Zurich by
Facet Publishing Production.
Printed and made in Great Britain by CPI Group (UK) Ltd, Croydon,
CR0 4YY.

Contents

List of figures ix

Preface xi

1 An introduction to social media 1
So what is 'social media'? 2
Complexity and simplicity 4
Cloud-based versus computer-based 5
Browser-based or installed software 6
Solitary or crowd-based 8
Communication...9
Where is data now? 10
Validating content 12
Control through the website, or dispersed 12
Web/internet/social search...13
Information tracked down, or brought to us 13
Getting it right or getting it quickly...14
Connection speeds and storage costs 15
Our roles 15
Web 1.0 was about limitations, social media is about freedom 16
Summary 16

2 Authority checking 17
Introduction 17
Facebook...19
Twitter 21
LinkedIn 23
Google properties 23
Blogs 25
Other ways to check authority 26
Summary 27
URLs mentioned in this chapter 28

3 Guiding tools..**31**
  Introduction 31
  Home or start pages..32
  Pearltrees 36
  Google customized search engines 38
  Bookmarking packages...39
  Blending bookmarks into a social media strategy 41
  Summary 42
  URLs mentioned in this chapter 43

4 Current awareness and selective dissemination of
   information resources **45**
  Introduction 45
  Let the networks take the strain! 46
  Tablet-based applications..47
  Web-based curation tools 48
  News curation by e-mail 54
  Summary 54
  URLs mentioned in this chapter 56

5 Presentation tools **59**
  Introduction 59
  Additions to PowerPoint...59
  Prezi 62
  Interactive presentations 64
  Timeline packages..66
  Easy-to-create presentations 67
  Animated presentations 69
  Summary 70
  URLs mentioned in this chapter 70

6 Teaching and training **73**
  Introduction 73
  Screencasting 73
  Screencapture 76
  Interactive training: Google+ Hangouts 78
  Interactive training: other resources 80
  MOOCs 81
  Advantages and disadvantages of e-learning 82
  Summary 83
  URLs mentioned in this chapter 83

7 Communication..**85**
  Introduction 85
  'Just the facts' 86
  Twitter 87
  Facebook...93
  LinkedIn 97

Google+ communities 98
Blogging 98
Chat rooms 103
Wikis 104
Sticky note software...105
Google Docs..107
Distributing your content 107
Summary 108
URLs mentioned in this chapter 108

8 Marketing and promotion – the groundwork 111
Introduction 111
Blending your social media presences..................................111
Getting past the organization roadblock 115
Search engine optimization (SEO) 121
Location 122
Consumer rather than creator 123
Monitoring tools..124
Summary 125
URLs mentioned in this chapter 126

9 Marketing and promotion – the practicalities..............127
Introduction 127
Images 127
Photographic manipulation 131
Make images more exciting...132
Infographics 136
Podcasting 137
Video 140
Augmented reality...142
Summary 143
URLs mentioned in this chapter 144

10 Creating a social media policy 147
Introduction 147
Why an organization needs a social media policy..........................148
Defining social media 149
Social media policies for specific tools..150
Personal versus professional 152
The chain of command...154
Dealing with criticism 156
Do's and don'ts..156
Legal issues 157
How often should a policy be reviewed? 158
Summary 158
URLs mentioned in this chapter 158

Appendix: Social media disasters **159**
 'United Breaks Guitars' 159
 Never seconds 160
 Tweeting from the wrong handle 161
 Employees being stupid 161
 Turning a negative into a positive..............................162
 Watch the news, don't just react to it 163
 Don't pick a fight with the internet!............................164
 Summary 164

Index **167**

List of figures

1.1 Google Ngram Viewer 3
2.1 Screenshot of a Google result for Danny Sullivan 24
2.2 The author's Google+ profile..25
3.1 The author's Symbaloo home page...32
3.2 An RSS feed pulled from the BBC News website 33
3.3 The Symbaloo tiles for The Guardian newspaper 33
3.4 The author's Pearltree collection 36
3.5 The Search Engines Pearltree 37
3.6 Social Media search engines on Pearltrees 37
4.1 A screenshot from the author's Scoop.it! page...............................49
4.2 The Scoop.it! bookmarklet in action..50
4.3 The Paper.li newspaper, 'The Phil Bradley Daily' 52
5.1 A Knovio presentation by the author 60
5.2 Prezi presentation on social media for music students 63
5.3 The Meograph menu...66
5.4 A Wright brothers timeline made with Timeglider 67
5.5 The Powtoon dashboard 70
6.1 Windows toolbar with Snipping tool icon 76
6.2 Elements of the Snipping tool...77
7.1 Essex Libraries Facebook page 95
7.2 A Padlet wall in action...106
8.1 The author's Twitter avatar with associated 'twibbons'.................114
8.2 The Topeka and Shawnee County Public Library Foursquare
    entry 123
9.1 An example of a badge created in BigHugeLabs............................128
9.2 A trading card created using BigHugeLabs.....................................128
9.3 A Tagxedo word cloud of Sherlock Holmes 131

Preface

I first discovered social media by accident in about 2005. Of course, I'd been blogging for a few years by then, and found blogs a really useful way to keep up to date with what was happening in the areas that interested me. However, I started to notice a sudden influx of new tools that internet users could use to add content to their existing websites, to produce their own guides and so on. I also heard rumblings of a resource called Facebook, and shortly afterwards, some bizarre thing called Twitter. As I thought that some of these tools might be of interest to the information community I started to collect them and created a list on my website of about 100. I blogged once to tell readers that I had done this and within a week I was getting 50,000 hits a day on my website, and it was at about then that I realized there was a really large seismic shift in the way that the internet was evolving. Of course in those days we knew it as Web 2.0, and indeed in 2007 I wrote a title for Facet called *How to Use Web 2.0 in Your Library*.

Thankfully we quickly dropped the 'Web 2.0' terminology and moved on. Social media has developed since those early days and it has indeed changed the internet that we know, but it's also had a huge effect on the way that the world in general works and communicates. People are realizing that they have more power than ever before to create their own content, to share material with other people, to hold companies to account or indeed perhaps change the political structures of the country that they live in. Social media tools change the way that we get our news, and indeed, we can now become citizen journalists ourselves, but with that power also comes the responsibility of using it correctly. Some people have found to their cost and liberty that they're not as free to say what they want as they perhaps thought they were.

However, 'social media' as a term is not something I find particularly helpful, since it comes with a great deal of baggage, much of it heaped on by the mainstream media. As you'll discover as you read this book, I have tried to look at social media in a rather different way. Rather than focusing on tools such as Facebook, Twitter and Pinterest I have looked at what activities information professionals carry out, and to see how these tools can assist them in those activities – how they can be done quicker, faster, cheaper and more effectively.

People often say to me things such as 'I want to have a Twitter account' or 'We need to be on Facebook', and if you're coming to this title hoping that I'm going to tell you that yes, you absolutely need to be using various tools, you may be a little disappointed. However, if you want to know how to communicate more effectively, how to teach people different skills, or how to market and promote your service, then I hope that you'll find what you need between these covers.

I have written this book so that it can either be read sequentially or, if you wish, to just dip in and out according to your interests or requirements. However, let's take a quick run through of each chapter in turn.

Chapter 1 is an introduction to social media. For a subject that is constantly in the news, referred to everywhere online, and something that most of us use on a daily basis (or dislike enough not to use on a daily basis!) a clear definition is hard to come by. For many people, it's all about the tools, but as we'll see in the chapter, I'm much more interested in activities rather than tools.

Chapter 2 deals with the thorny issue of authority checking. An advantage of social media tools is that anyone can become a creator of content, and an equal disadvantage is that it seems most people do. It's becoming much harder to sift the good from the bad, particularly when people present clever hoaxes as fact to promote a television show or simply to increase their own 'fame' on the net. Information professionals are more needed than ever in a social media world, and this chapter goes into detail on the whys and wherefores.

Chapter 3 – guiding tools. Once you have found good material it's worth holding onto it, and providing users with access to that material is a key role that we can take on. As a profession we are one of the most trusted, and we should capitalize on that, not only to help our patrons and clients, but to promote our own skills and abilities.

Chapter 4 covers current awareness and the selective dissemination of information. There's no point in actually spending time creating all this great content, finding good quality material and establishing guiding tools to it if we're not actually telling people about it. There are plenty of ways of doing this quickly and effectively, and this chapter deals with them in some detail.

Chapter 5 looks at the difficult question of presentations. We all suffer poor presentations, and most of us have given one or two bad ones in our time. However, it's really not necessary; these days there are some excellent alternatives to 'death by PowerPoint'.

Chapter 6 is focused on teaching and training. This is a role that more and more information specialists are having to take on, and for many people who haven't done it before it can be quite daunting. There's no need to worry, however, since the tools that are available make the whole task not only easy but quite fun.

Chapter 7 concentrates on communication. If we do anything as a profession, it's communicate. Whatever we do or find, or however we answer a question for a library member, we have to get that information to them. There are plenty of ways of doing that, and also telling people what else we're doing, as you'll see in this chapter.

Chapter 8 is directed towards the concepts behind marketing and promotion. Not only is it necessary to decide what you want to do, and who you want to market it towards, but you may also have to fight the powers that be to allow you to do it, using these 'new-fangled' ideas. This chapter addresses some of those issues.

Chapter 9 then moves the discussion forward onto the practicalities of marketing and promotion; the hows, whys and whens.

Finally, in Chapter 10 you'll have an opportunity to consider the things that must be taken into account when creating a social media policy.

In the Appendix, as a reward for all of the hard work, I've taken a look at a few social media disasters, and how they could have been avoided if a sensible policy had been in place.

It's worth mentioning that this title isn't really a 'how-to' book, in the sense that I don't go into a lot of detail on how to use specific social media tools, or how to set up accounts and so on. There are plenty of guides already available that do that for you; if you are in any doubt, take a quick peep on YouTube and you'll be bombarded with them. Second, tools change on a regular basis, and what might well be an accurate description today may not be so accurate when you come to read it yourself. Instead, I've chosen to focus on what activities you can do better, differently or more effectively in the future, with examples of tools that can help you do that.

I've also tried not to narrow down the focus of the book to a particular type of library or information centre, either. It doesn't really matter if we look at the jobs and roles of school librarians, public librarians or government or corporate librarians – they are all involved in similar activities. It's true that their audiences will be very different, but all information professionals need to be concerned with the authority of their sources, and all of them have to communicate information to their different groups. While the environment is different, the fundamentals stay the same. You'll also notice that I try to vary the words that I use to describe the people that you work with; your clients, customers, users, patrons, members or any other terms that a thesaurus can turn up. This has been deliberate on my part, since I don't believe that one term fits all, and I don't particularly like any one term. 'Clients' and 'customers' does tend to imply that the role of the information professional is transaction-based (usually financial) and in most instances that isn't the case. However, some librarians do bill different departments for their time, so it can be a valid description. I know that a lot of American readers of this book will cringe at the widely used British term 'user', since there is the potential for drug-related associations, but I actually quite like the idea of people being addicted to books and libraries. Similarly British users are going to get annoyed at the 'patrons' term, since it's simply never used in this country. So while you're tutting over one term, sympathize with a colleague elsewhere in the world who will be tutting over another. Finally I've used 'member' quite often, and it's my personal preference. If a library service is about and for anything, it's the people who make use of it. A 'library member' implies to me someone who buys into a particular service, not particularly in terms of money, but in terms of time, enthusiasm, trust and belief in the services that are provided by professionals. However, if you prefer some other term, do feel free to use your own global 'delete and replace' in your head, and accept my apologies!

There is of course an inevitable problem when writing a book, and that is that it's out of date. While writing this preface, I'm already aware of things that I have to go back and change, and there will have to be continual updates until the book goes to press. There's very little that I can do about that, of course, but I can at least try and mitigate the annoyance for readers. I'll be producing a short video for every chapter, which will be hosted on the Facet Publishing YouTube channel, and there will be a link to each of them at the end of the chapter concerned. Each video will be a little different – one might be me introducing new ideas or tools that have been created after the book has been published, another might address issues that have changed, while a third may be a 'how-to' type of video. You'll have to look through each video in turn to find out exactly what I'm covering, because at this stage even I don't know, and it's quite probable that I'll replace videos with new ones through the lifetime of the title.

Every effort has been made to contact the holders of copyright material reproduced in this text, and thanks are due to them for permission to reproduce the material indicated. If there are any queries please contact the publisher.

Finally I'd like to thank all my friends and colleagues who helped me with this title, either directly with suggestions, thoughts, ideas or cups of tea, or indirectly by pointing me towards useful tools, or made me think harder about various subjects. This is dedicated with love to some very important people in my life: Bee, Jill, Gaynor, Marian and Sam.

Phil Bradley

CHAPTER 1

An introduction to social media

The Jetsons – a futuristic cartoon created in the 1960s and set 100 years later – told the story of the eponymous family and their day-to-day life. George Jetson worked two days a week, for an hour each day, and he commuted to his office in an aerocar that looked vaguely like a flying saucer. He would fly through the air, along with everyone else on their daily commute, and when he got to work his aerocar would pack down into the size of a suitcase until it was time for the trip home. There's also a cut scene in the opening where Mrs Jetson takes Mr Jetson's wallet, leaving him with the $10 note that he was originally offering her. Hanna-Barbera looked into the future and were able to tell that things were going to be different – we were all going to have aerocars, but they were unable to take the next leap, which was to further extrapolate that we probably wouldn't need to physically go to work.

You may be wondering why I'm beginning a book on social media with a brief description of an elderly cartoon series, but what is interesting isn't the cartoon itself, but the attitudes shown towards the future, and how things were going to be different – or stay very much the same. I run courses on social media on a regular basis, and it's interesting to see how delegates view the concept of social media when we begin. Some people see social media as a whole new world, in which everything has changed, or at least has the potential to change; the tools to them are like the aerocar, promising excitement and difference. Other people on the same course will have had experience of some tools and will say that nothing has actually changed; as with the aerocar, Mr Jetson still has to go to work and put the car somewhere until he's ready for the trip home.

My delegates' views of social media can therefore be seen in exactly the same way that Hanna-Barbera gazed into the future; everything changed but paradoxically everything remained the same. There is a very great temptation to view the future in the way that we have viewed the past; it's easy, comforting and doesn't take very much hard work. However, it's also the wrong thing to do. Eric Shinseki, a retired US Army general, is quoted as saying 'If you dislike change, you're going to dislike irrelevance even more.' In order to understand exactly what social media is, the extent to which it is different from what we have had in the past, and how it will change libraries, it's necessary to compare and contrast the 'old' way of doing things (I'll leave it up to you to define 'old' – for some it may only be a few minutes while for others it will be years) with the way in which things work in the new world of social media.

So what is 'social media'?

It's impossible not to hear references to the term these days. If your colleagues are not talking about the social media presence the company has, you'll be hearing the media making a huge fuss about the latest scandal, or your children talking about something that makes very little sense, but relates in some way to them talking to their friends using an app you have never heard of. Before we can get anywhere, therefore, we have to have a clear indication of exactly what we (and when I say 'we', in the context of this book I mean 'I') are talking about.

In 2005 I started to notice that there was a minor explosion in the functionality that could be added to web pages, to turn them from an entirely static screen full of information to a jigsaw where information from a news site, for example, could be dropped directly onto a page and then updated real-time. I saw that people were able to create chat rooms quickly and easily, or share documents with each other without requiring a qualification in computer programming. In short, life was very quickly becoming easier for everyone and much more could be done on the net. Furthermore, there was a small little start-up company called Facebook which was really just for students to chat to each other. We also had LinkedIn, a place that you could look for a new job, or MySpace, which was a very exciting innovation, allowing people to share their ideas, thoughts, opinions and hobbies.

I decided to create a simple one-page listing of all of these new tools, and this was quickly picked up by the Digg bookmarking service; by the end of the first week that the page was available it was getting 50,000 hits per day. It was at that point I thought to myself 'Hmm, I might be onto something here'.

Over the course of the next few months the phrase 'Web 2.0' really started to take off, to the point that just about everything seemed to have 2.0 tacked on the end of it. The phrase did serve a purpose over the next few years, but it did bring with it some baggage – rather too technical a phrase for what was really a change in the way that people were starting to use the internet. People began to look at the rise of sites such as MySpace and Facebook, as well as LinkedIn, and as a result the current term, 'social media' became the preferred one. If we take a look at the Google Ngram Viewer (Figure 1.1) for the two phrases we'll see that 'social media' as a phrase really began to take off in 2005, and has remained the dominant term ever since.

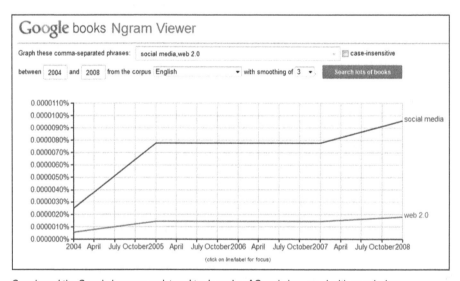

Google and the Google logo are registered trademarks of Google Inc., used with permission

Figure 1.1 Google Ngram Viewer

In all honesty, I'm not entirely sure if the phrase has helped or hindered the use of tools that are generally regarded as being an integral part of the phenomenon. The mainstream media tends to emphasize the 'social' element of the phrase, and concomitant with that is the suggestion that it's about friends, having fun and for pleasure, rather than work. Taking into account the inevitable sensationalism of stories of out-of-control parties, stalkers and vigilantes, it's not surprising that some employers want to steer clear of any association with this internet development. My personal preference is to use the term 'stuff', as in 'there's lots of stuff out there that you can use to make your job easier and more effective'. However, I'm aware that simply using 'stuff' isn't really going to be enough of a definition, so let's look in a little more detail at the difference between the internet as it was, and as it is now.

Complexity and simplicity

The internet used to be a far more complicated place in some respects. In order to share information you had to be able to create a website, which meant a working knowledge of the basics of HTML (HyperText Markup Language), the money to get a domain name and web space, the ability to FTP (copy across) your files, and then some idea of how best to create content that would rank highly with search engines. Moreover, given that a lot of website creation was taken over by web editing teams or technical support departments, it meant that the majority of people really didn't have much of an outlet for their own thoughts, opinions and creativity, other than using their own weblogs, of course.

Weblog software did however point the way forward for most of us; authoring packages such as Blogger and LiveJournal, which had been around since about 2000, showed people that they didn't have to have all of that knowledge. A simple (and in most cases free) blogging platform meant that people could create their own blogs on whatever subjects interested them, and start to share their enthusiasm or expertise. Nowadays, of course, it is simplicity itself to create a group on Facebook or Google+, start a wiki or have your own television channel hosted by YouTube.

The ability for people to create their own user-generated content has had very far-reaching effects, and it's not an exaggeration to say that it has changed (and continues to change) the way that society develops, from protesters communicating by Blackberry Messenger (which now seems almost quaint) to people using apps and their smartphones to become citizen journalists. This is even before we start to look at the sheer amount of content that is produced and disseminated on the internet every day. For now, in this simple overview, let's limit ourselves to the idea that social media tools allow us all to create, rather than just consume. It is, however, something that I'd like to put into a little more perspective. In order to gain an indication of the enormous scale of the content that we are producing, a few illustrative statistics should suffice. In September 2013 Twitter's data showed that 200 million users sent over 400 million tweets daily. Five new Facebook profiles are created every second, and 300 million photographs are uploaded to the social network every day. There are currently over 2 million LinkedIn groups, with 8000 new groups created every week (figures from www.business2community.com/infographics/social-media-nutshell-0781415#!xvFdD).

Cloud-based versus computer-based

Most of us used to store our content on our desktop machines, or on office intranets, which is really a big version of the same thing. With the ease of use of CD ROM and DVD technology it became easier to take our information with us. The ubiquitous nature of USB drives has extended this even further, and most of us will be able to put our hands on several of these devices within seconds. While this does make our lives easier, it still means that we are tied to our data physically, or at least, it did. Now, however, we have access to 'the cloud', which is to say unlimited storage space on servers online. If I want to give a presentation I can simply upload it onto one of several presentation-sharing websites, and make it available for people to view, embed or download. My bookmarks are stored online using any one of a number of services, and the system can be automated so that if I tweet a link to a site it's automatically copied to my bookmarking service. It also means that I can share my bookmarks with other people (mostly people that I don't actually know) with ease. I have created YouTube training videos which are stored on their servers and I can curate subject areas of interest using yet more tools. As I'm writing this chapter my computer is taking an entire back-up of my hard drive and placing it onto a cloud-based storage system.

We are finally moving into an environment where the artefact – the book, the CD or even the USB stick, are becoming redundant. As long as I have access to the net (which I agree is sometimes a big ask), I have access to all of my data, and I can choose who I want to share that with. Not only does it make my life easier without having to worry about carrying about data back-ups with me, it means that we can far more easily work with colleagues, since content is available to be shared and used 24/7. These tools mean that I can take a photograph on my smartphone and it's almost instantly available on my desktop. I can start reading a chapter of a book on a Kindle on the train and finish it on my tablet in bed at night. We can all become citizen journalists, sharing our videos with the world seconds after they have been recorded, creating a new immediacy, and redefining what 'news' actually means.

Browser-based or installed software

When you bought a new computer it was common practice to buy a suite of software to go with it, and if you were using a Windows-based operating system that usually meant something like Microsoft Office. Moreover, if you needed a particular job done, such as video conferencing or sharing access to a computer across a network, you had to buy a specific piece of software. Software was seldom cheap, and to justify the price the manufacturer would provide lots of extra functionality that the vast majority of us would never use. I suspect that it's only a very small number of people using Microsoft Word who have ever used much in the way of page layout functions, references or mailing lists. Over the course of time users would get patches to their software and then a new version would be made available for people to buy, and the whole cycle would begin again.

Everyone bought into the concept that software cost money – a lot of money – and that there was a particular cycle of updating and purchasing that went with it. It meant that people who were in charge of buying software products had to make sure that the tool was suitable for the job, and that everyone had to use exactly the same piece of software to make life easier for technical support staff. It also meant buying into a particular operating system, and accepting a particular view that the tool was the important thing. After all, staff had to be trained on it, or follow a steep learning curve, budgets had to be agreed, and the package had to be everything to everyone.

However, social media-based tools have turned this notion on its head. Many of the tools that people create now are entirely free at point of use. This can be difficult for some people to really get to grips with, and a question that I am often asked is 'if this is all free software, how do people make money?' There are a number of answers to this question. Sometimes people are just not that interested in making money; some people just like creating software and get pleasure from other people using it. Others will provide full access to the software, but with some sort of limit on it; a maximum number of files, or storage space for example. Others are hopeful that if lots of people use their product and are complimentary about it one of the big companies will come in and buy them out. While the financial approach differs, what remains the same is that in order to be used the software has to be of a high standard; anything less than that and people will go elsewhere. The idea of brand or product loyalty is beginning to die a death now. The important thing to bear in mind isn't the tool, it's the activity. If I want to send a large file to someone, there are lots of tools out there that I can use; I really don't care which one it happens to be as long as it does the job that I want it to. I may or may not use that tool again, or another one may take my attention instead.

Consequently we can now rethink our attitudes towards software. A well known aphorism is that people who buy drills don't want a drill, they want a hole in their wall, and much the same can be said of computer software. It's far too easy to say 'we need a Twitter account' with the reason behind it being 'everyone else has one' but really the social media savvy will be saying 'we want to communicate more effectively – what tool will help us do that?' There is a reasonable and justifiable concern that free software means unreliable software, and I can certainly provide examples of when free tools have ceased operation. However, they generally make it clear that the resource is being closed down and will provide ways that people can move their data from one tool to another, and if they don't, the competition certainly will! To balance that view though, I can also provide examples of software that hasn't been updated because the company selling it has gone out of business. After all, if we cannot trust the liquidity of banking institutions these days, we certainly can't trust individual companies.

My advice therefore is to ignore the tool and concentrate on the activity first and foremost. When you're clear in what you want to achieve, then find a tool that does what you need. Next, check out the competition (there's always competition, irrespective of the resource), and see which one(s) colleagues use. If the tool ceases to do what is required of it, simply move to a different tool; you do not owe anyone brand loyalty, as I mentioned before; it is one of the victims of the way in which we now work online.

So if the tool isn't important – what about the browser? Any good tool should work within any browser, so you should be prepared to try out any number of them. Obvious suggestions are Firefox, Chrome and Internet Explorer, but there's also Safari for Apple-based products, TOR (The Onion

Router) for privacy, Opera and so on. Indeed, forget the idea that it's necessary to just choose one browser – since you're not paying for them, have several available to use. In fact, it makes a lot of sense to do exactly that – have one browser that you use to log into your Facebook and Google accounts (for example) and another browser that you can use in an anonymous mode for the times when privacy and confidentiality are paramount. If you add to this the point that each browser has access to different apps and bolt-ons, it actually makes sense to tailor browsers for different purposes.

Solitary or crowd-based

The internet – and indeed computing generally – used to be quite an isolated and isolating place; we're all aware of the films that have the solitary young man alone in his room with nothing but his computer for company before he goes on a horrific killing spree. I wouldn't quite want to go to those extremes, but I would go so far as to say that it used to be very difficult to share things online, be they ideas, thoughts and opinions, or bookmarks, files or presentations.

Social media has, of course, opened this out now so that everyone who has access to a computer or mobile device and the internet can share and interact with other people across the globe in ways that were previously unimaginable. Everyone was locked into his or her own silo, but now we can share our wisdom (such as it is) with the crowds. I no longer have to try and work out what would be a good restaurant to eat in when I visit a new city: I can simply go into Facebook and run a search to see which restaurants my friends have recommended. If I am considering staying in a particular hotel it makes sense to check with an online review site to see if it really is as good as the website makes out. If I need ideas or opinions on a subject I just go onto Twitter, ask my question, and within the space of half an hour or so helpful colleagues will have pointed me in the right direction.

There are advantages and disadvantages to a system where everyone can share indiscriminately. One good aspect is that the individual is no longer alone; if he or she is being bullied or ignored by a large corporate, crowdsourcing of ideas or harnessing outrage can help to right a wrong. Even something as seemingly innocuous as watching a YouTube video can make a difference, as Canadian musician Dave Carroll found out. He had the unfortunate experience that his guitar was broken during a trip on

United Airlines in 2008, and had poor customer service. He wrote and produced a song, *United Breaks Guitars* which he put onto YouTube, whereupon it became an immediate hit, as well as a terrible public relations disaster for the airline. For the full story, see the Appendix, p. 159. In another case a graphic designer known as HiddenEloise found that her work had been used without permission by a well known design company. People on Twitter flexed their muscles and a media storm quickly blew up, resulting in recognition by the company of the designer's work.

Unfortunately, however, it is all too easy for false information to spread widely via social media, and any number of celebrities are mourned, while still healthy and alive. For one very brief evening back in August 2012 it appeared (wrongly) that a lion was loose in Essex, a county in eastern England. People were tweeting sightings of the lion, making jokes about it, postings photographs and so on. The police contacted circuses to see if any lions were missing, the RSPCA got involved and while a good time was had by all, resources could have been put to much better use.

The lesson is clear – just because something is reported on social media does not make it true or accurate. Hundreds of thousands of people can be wrong, they can be whipped up into a frenzy and jokes can turn into facts and facts can be misinterpreted. As a result, the role of the information professional in this situation is clear – to ignore the numbers, track the story back to its origins, sift the facts from the fiction and then make that information available as appropriate.

Communication

Communicating on the internet used to be simplicity itself – you had an e-mail address and sent people e-mail. This developed to the point that we then had mailing lists that we could use to share content back and forth between larger numbers of people. Other early developments were IRC or Internet Relay Chat, which allowed for real-time typed chat back and forth between groups of people in specially designed chatrooms, and newsgroups or USENET – a worldwide distributed discussion system. However, despite these alternatives, e-mail was still the major way that people would send and receive information. It is expected that the total number of e-mail accounts worldwide is going to increase from nearly 3.9 billion accounts in 2013 to almost 5 billion by the end of 2017. It is also estimated the total number of e-mails sent/received per day in 2014 is 191.4

billion, an increased growth rate of 5% over the previous year (www.radicati.com/wp/wp-content/uploads/2013/04/Email-Statistics-Report-2013-2017-Executive-Summary.pdf).

While the growth in e-mail remains quite astonishing, it is matched by the number of other ways that we can now contact people and share information with them. For example: if my friend has a smartphone I can text her, and share links, multimedia content and more:

- Most of my friends are on Facebook, so it's easy to simply message them, or if they are online at the same time, we can chat, or start a video conversation.
- Similarly, Google provides me with the ability to set up a Google+ Hangout and chat with my colleagues.
- Several of my friends are keen photographers, and they use Flickr to post and share their photographs, mainly on a daily basis. It's simplicity itself to just go to Flickr and send them a memo.
- Some colleagues are on LinkedIn, so I can post them a message, or if they are active in a LinkedIn group, I can leave a comment in the form of a post.
- Obviously I can go onto Twitter and message friends, or send private direct messages.
- Chatroom software exists in abundance: it doesn't require software installation, or even registration – you can just open a chatroom, invite some friends and off you go.

I could easily go on, but I'm sure you get the point; communicating within the 'new' internet – with real-time media – is no longer the simple system that it once was. In actual fact it's far more complicated than it has ever been, and it's important to make sure that you choose the right tool at the right time.

Where is data now?

In the past, if you wanted to know about an organization or a company it was relatively easy – you would simply go to your favourite search engine, type in the name of the company and then click on the link to their website. Of course, you can still do that, but now it's more important to think of exactly what it is that you want to do, with what sort of information. For example, if you simply need their address or phone number, getting that via the website is still the obvious course of action. However, if you wish to talk to a representative of the company is it better to contact them via their Twitter account (and if so, which one, if they have several), or their Facebook page? Perhaps they have a profile on Pinterest, or they may be active on some other social networking site.

The information that people can make available now has not only increased exponentially, but the places where you can find the information has similarly increased. A couple of years ago the National Trust (a cultural and historical body in the UK) produced, in conjunction with a television company, an interesting programme ('The Manor Reborn') on the restoration of a run-down property. I watched it with interest, but had lots of questions about what was being done to the property, so I visited the National Trust website. All that was able to tell me was that the programme was on television at a particular time on a particular channel; not terribly useful, since I already had that information. However, I then went to the National Trust Facebook page and the top update on the site mentioned the programme and pointed out that several experts were online at that moment, waiting to take questions and get involved in discussions around issues that the programme aired. Doubtless I could also have got involved via Twitter with an appropriate hashtag as well.

So as a consumer of content it's increasingly necessary to spread the net much wider to get access to all sorts of information that's made available in different places. As creators of content, we are in a similar position. A dozen or so years ago I would write an article and share it directly on my website for people to view it. Then in 2003 I started writing my own blog and I was faced with the dilemma of what to put where – exacerbated by creating a second blog a short while after. I can now tweet material that I think is interesting, share it on a news curation or magazine site such as Scoop.it!, pin images to my Pinterest account, let my friends and colleagues see it via Facebook or Google+ updates, update my Flickr account with new photographs; the list is almost endless. I then also have to decide if I am going to cross-reference this material to other resources; if I tweet something, should I also share it on Facebook, annoying the people who follow me in both places? What about those on Facebook who don't follow me on Twitter, though? A particular skill in using social media is to know where to publish material, in what format (a long blog post or a short tweet for example), to which group(s) of people, and when this process should take place. The blessing of real-time media is also the curse; multiplying sources of content multiplies the work we need to do to find or publish our own content.

Validating content

Hard on the heels of finding information in a wide variety of places is the increasing need to check its validity. In the print days, this was simple; who was the publisher, what was their reputation, who was the author, what had they previously published and who cited them, and when was the material published? The internet gave rise to a whole different set of problems, but this could in many ways be overcome by a careful consideration of the website that the material was found on. Was the address one of the top-level domains, such as an .edu or .gov site, and which country did it come from? However, with social media we quickly found ourselves back in the bad old days of frontier life – few rules and regulations. Was the person who had a certain Twitter handle actually the celebrity that you thought it was? Is the Facebook offer that you see from a particular supermarket really genuine? Is some bizarre happening reported by people on the internet nothing more than a hoax perpetrated by some celebrity? The role of the information professional is going to be increasingly important in the future for sorting out what resources are accurate, truthful and relevant from those that are a waste of time.

Control through the website, or dispersed

This is a problem for many companies that have grown up with the idea that the website is the be-all and end-all of their involvement on the internet. Everything that they do, from providing access to company reports, publications, access to customer support, details on new products and so on has always gone through the website. This is now no longer the case, as social media tools are taking over a lot of the responsibility for that work. One only has to look at advertisements on the television or in the local press to see that more and more companies are pointing people to their Facebook or Twitter presence, rather than the website. We will always need websites of course, but the way in which they will be used in the future is going to change rapidly. In order to communicate with users or customers, it's necessary to develop social media accounts, and to go to where the conversations are taking place.

The particular issue that faces middle and senior management of course is that they realize that they no longer have control – of either the content or the message. However, that control was only ever illusory at the best of times, since people would always share information on organizations by e-mail, mailing lists or word of mouth. Social media has just exacerbated that situation.

Web/internet/social search

We often hear the irritating phrase 'it's all on Google'. Of course, it's never been all on Google, since while Google indexes trillions of pages, it's unable to index databases, information behind paywalls, content that authors don't want indexed, and so on. The rise of user-generated content has simply taken this to the next level. While Google is amazing in what it can do, even the search giant has limitations. YouTube videos are uploaded at the rate of 100 hours per minute, and Twitter processes between 400 million and 600 million tweets per day, to give you just two examples. There is no way that a single search engine can keep up with that level of output, so it's necessary to start looking at specialist social media search engines that can find the information that we need from blogs, comments on blogs, microblogging, photographs, video, and so on. Furthermore, Google has introduced its own social network, Google+, and this has had an impact on the way in which search results can be viewed, with a greater emphasis on people and organizations that have a G+ account. Meanwhile, Bing is working in conjunction with Facebook to bring in information from a user's friends, and Facebook itself is working hard to provide users with a superior search experience based upon their interests and those of their friends.

Information tracked down, or brought to us

Long gone are the days when we had to go out and find the information that we needed on a regular basis. Of course, we still need to track down the information that we are asked for, but the content that we need continually updated on a day-to-day basis, or developments in an area that interests us, can now be brought to us, saving time and providing more efficiency.

There are plenty of tools out there which do this job for us – the traditional RSS newsreaders, home or start pages, curation tools, resources that create magazines tailored to our personal exact interests – all are helping to spin a web for us where we sit at the centre. We can now spend more of our time sifting through content to find what we need and discarding the rest instead of hunting it down in the first place.

Getting it right or getting it quickly

Now this is not an either/or situation, of course – the date of the Battle of Hastings is never going to change, and if you provide someone with the answer '1065' you're just wrong. What I mean here is that there is a tendency towards making sure that everything possible has been done to check out a particular tool or resource, for example. When I am training, and showing delegates a particular tool, a common question is 'Who else is using this? We can't be the first.' There is a danger that if you wait too long for exactly the right tool, that may never happen, and the opportunity to get the information to the user passes.

The activity is the key element here; if I want to send a large file to someone for instance, that's exactly what I want to do. I don't particularly care which of the dozens of resources I use to do it, I just need the file sent. There is an understandable temptation to remain loyal to a particular product or tool, and that makes sense if you have paid money for it, or invested a lot of staff time in training. However, the days of loyalty are very long gone now, and your responsibility is towards your library members. Use the tool that will get the job done. If that tool is still there tomorrow, then that's great, use it again, and if it isn't, use something else instead.

In the past we had to focus on the tools, because they were expensive, and we had to get the tool to work as hard as possible. Consequently, the tool helped to define the activity; if you wanted to create a poster you would look at the functionality that Microsoft Word gave you for example, because that's the tool you had. With all of the resources that are now available, there are plenty of finely honed tools that create fantastic posters, far superior to anything that a word processing package could provide.

In essence – the tool is less important than the activity, and the activity should always define which tool or type of tool you use, not the other way around. Your members will expect to get the material or information that they need quickly, and it matters far less to them exactly how they get it.

Connection speeds and storage costs

In the past, the technical issues of connection speed and the cost of storing content online meant that far more work was done on desktop computers, and more latterly laptops. However, with many people now owning and using tablet devices and smartphones, storing their content in the cloud, these concerns are – for users in many countries – a thing of the past. We can now store everything that we need online; presentations can be made available on file-sharing sites, obviating the need to take presentations on physical media such as DVDs or thumbdrives. It also means that it's far easier to share content than ever before, and in many different formats – podcasts and video being obvious examples, but we shouldn't forget the newer resources such as augmented reality apps that sit on our smartphones.

Our roles

In the 'Web 1.0' world it was reasonably easy to settle ourselves into specific roles – librarian, researcher, author, reader, journalist, teacher, and so on. However, now that everyone can create and contribute, these traditional roles are beginning to fall apart. If I see an event happening in front of me I can video it, upload it and tweet about it there and then. I have become a 'citizen journalist'. We can all be book reviewers or film critics with our own channels on YouTube or pages on Facebook. It's much easier to teach people using webinars, screencasts, or one-on-one training via webcam.

Looking at this from a broader canvas, we are no longer restricted to watching television at particular periods of time, given all of the on-demand resources that are available to us. Indeed, why watch television at all, when we have tablets and smartphones available? Our role as passive viewer is becoming a thing of the past as we can choose what to watch, when we watch it, and how we discuss it with our friends afterwards.

We can still purchase printed materials and while we'll still do that, of course, the concept of news is changing, and personalized news feeds, culling content from people we follow on Twitter and Facebook, as well as other subject areas of interest, are becoming more important. This leads onto a second issue here, which is 'who is producing the news?' In the past our news has been pre-chosen, packaged and delivered for us by the national or local news, but now it's far easier to identify experts who cover subjects that interest us, and we can get our news from those people instead. Of course, we can also be those newscasters as well.

Web 1.0 was about limitations, social media is about freedom

For the majority of its 40+ years' existence, the internet has limited what people can do with it. Perhaps the best way to create content was via a website, and in order to do that it was necessary to understand HyperText Markup Language, File Transfer Protocols, search engine optimization, and so on. While USENET newsgroups and early blogging platforms helped people break away from those limitations it's only been in the last decade that the rise of user-generated content has exploded, giving everyone with access to the internet a chance to find their own voice.

Summary

Social media has changed the way in which society as a whole works, and more particularly the way that information professionals are able to do their jobs. While the focus is very often on the actual tools that we can use, Twitter, Facebook and the like are simply that – tools. In the wrong hands the best that can be achieved is nothing, since in order to use a tool it's necessary to understand how it can work, the uses that it can be put to, and the activities that it supports. The following chapters look in detail at various activities information professionals can take part in, and indeed are already taking part in, and the role that various different tools have in supporting this work.

Visit the Facet Publishing YouTube channel (www.youtube.com/user/facetpublishing) for Phil Bradley's video Introduction to Social Media for Creative Libraries.

CHAPTER 2

Authority checking

Introduction

A vital activity that information professionals have always undertaken is checking the validity of the content that they find, and warning or advising their enquirers. The publication date of a book, the bias of the newspaper, the expertise of the author, the respect accorded to the journal and the number of citations for the article are all standard criteria that have been used on a daily basis and, of course, are still used.

With the increasing importance of the internet it was necessary to come to grips with an entirely new way of assessing the authority and validity of the content that appeared on the screen. The URL of a website with, for example, a .gov.uk domain trumped that of a more casual .co.uk. In the early days of the expansion of the internet there was a real Wild West attitude at large, with people registering any domain names that they could get their hands on, in the hope of selling it back to the 'rightful owner'. I recall some enterprising soul buying up various .co.uk domains using the names of different universities, then selling them on for a quick profit. However, that particularly lucrative trade didn't last too long before the lawyers and courts got involved. It's still an interesting area, though, as new domain names are constantly being put into circulation, and we now face a plethora of new domain extensions such as .guru, .food, .wales, .finance and so on.

There are also plenty of fake or spoof websites in existence and in the main these are created simply for the humour of the situation. The Dihydrogen Monoxide Research Division, at www.dhmo.org is one such example, warning us about the dangers of a dangerous chemical otherwise known as 'water', or the delightful Dog Island, at www.thedogisland.com, which is a site that describes an island where dogs are free to roam and bark and play all day long while on their holidays. However, there are also rather more unsavoury sites, such as the one produced by a racist organization designed to criticize a particular civil rights leader, which constantly gets a high ranking in Google results. We have learned by trial, error and basic common sense not to trust the information that we find on the internet, and part of our job is to pass this wariness onto the people that we work with.

User-generated social media content has made the problem of authority and validity checking harder by several orders of magnitude. While we may reserve a certain amount of scepticism for 'facts' and stories that we see from sources that we don't know, we are generally far more trusting of the information that our friends share with us. Surely our friends, whom we know to be solid sensible people with more than their fair share of common sense, would never fall for a prank, even less pass it onto other people that they know? Unfortunately this kind of thinking makes inaccurate information much more prevalent than it's ever been before. Furthermore, celebrities or television hosts will use social media to create their own stories, complete with images or video, to craft something that they can then own up to on their shows, increasing their ratings. Other people will see a story and decide to run with it, just for the sake of humour – these are what are generally referred to as 'memes' and they often relate to things that are happening in the news. For example, when Germany knocked Brazil out of the World Cup Twitter users started posting jokes, links to videos and humorous images onto the site, which I suspect everyone except Brazilian supporters enjoyed. More seriously, back in early 2012 Twitter was abuzz with claims that Fidel Castro had died, and several tweets included faked photographs of him dead in a coffin. Sometimes rumours of this nature are deliberately spread in attempts to encourage people to click on links that then download viruses onto their systems. So, irrespective of the reasoning behind some claims on social media, it can be a very untrustworthy medium. Critics will use this to claim that nothing posted onto social media can really be trusted, but that view is as incorrect as the one at the other end of the spectrum, that because something is on the internet it must be right.

As information professionals, it's important that we're able to quickly sift out accurate content while dismissing material that is not only inappropriate, but which is also plain wrong. In this chapter I'll look at some of the things that we need to consider when checking the authority and validity of the information that's out there, paying particular attention to Facebook and Twitter.

Facebook

How many times do we see news items shared with us from our friends which claim that we cannot think of a country that doesn't have an 'e' in its name, or asking us to comment and share with the first word that we see in a word square. Or alternatively, asking us to comment with a particular word and to share, in order to see what happens next? Of course, if we take part and follow the instructions nothing ever happens, so we shrug our shoulders and move onto something else that catches our eye.

However, something is actually happening; it's just that we don't see it. Facebook uses a ranking system to decide what information to show us, and the position of different pages in search results; Google does exactly the same thing. However, while Google uses ranking criteria such as the number and quality of pages that link to a page, the position of search terms on the web page and so on, Facebook takes into account the number of likes and shares that updates get. So the more popular a page, the more chance there is that people will see it in their search results. The next step is that people can then sell the Facebook page that they have created for significant amounts of money, and of course the more likes and comments the page has, the more it can be sold for. In fact, there is even a page on Facebook called 'Fan Pages for Sale'! The new owner can then rebadge the page, delete all of the old information and postings and start using it for whatever purpose they wish. Facebook appears to have little interest in stopping this practice, because their interest is in making money from the adverts that people click on, so the more activity there is on the site, the more it profits them.

This is only one concern associated with Facebook, however; there are plenty more. Another type of status update you may see passed onto you by a friend or a colleague is one that appears to offer you the chance to win an iPad or some other luxury item by liking a particular page. This may well be associated with a reputable company, but again caution should be exercised. A page for the supermarket giant Tesco, called unsurprisingly 'Tesco' is not the same page as another one called 'Tesco.' and that final full stop is crucial, as Facebook views this as two entirely different pages. The keen shopper intent on a bargain will probably not notice this, which is the point of the exercise. They may have to follow a link to claim the chance to win the luxury item, but before they can, they have to fill out a questionnaire or survey. Once they have done that, they have to fill out another, then another and so on. The opportunity to register an interest never arrives, because this particular scam comes about because someone is paid to get surveys filled out, and the more of those that are completed, the more money they will earn. The individual who does the actual work however gets nothing, except frustration.

A third type of Facebook problem comes when well-meaning people will like a particular page because they are told that if the page gets a certain number of likes a child will have cancer treatment paid for them by Microsoft or some other large multinational company. This is, of course, nonsense and in most cases the particular child in question does not even exist. This type of scam preys on the kindness and generosity of people, but nonetheless causes problems for everyone else who has their own Facebook timeline cluttered up with these nonsensical postings.

So, what is the informed professional to do? Firstly, maintain a healthy level of scepticism over these postings. If it sounds too good to be true, then as the old saying goes, it probably is too good to be true. Check out the actual source page or fan group, in particular the number of comments and likes the page has. A popular site such as a supermarket will have millions of likes, with tens of thousands of people talking about it. Check to see the activity on the page, and in particular see when the page was initially created; anything in the last six months or so should perhaps be treated with some caution. Next, run a search yourself from the Facebook search box, and compare the page(s) that Facebook suggests to you with the one that links to the amazing offer. Finally, it's worth checking out some of the sites that highlight these fake or spoof pages; two in particular that you can visit are Hoax-Slayer, at www.hoax-slayer.com and Snopes, the urban rumour site, at www.snopes.com. Having ascertained that the page or offer in question is a fake, it's worth contacting the person who posted it to let them know, and also suggest that they delete their original posting.

Now, you may well question the reason for doing all of this, and my response is that – as an information professional – we have duties and responsibilities to the people that we work with. Not just our immediate friends, relations and colleagues, but the wider public as well, and helping them raise their own level of awareness, increasing their own digital literacy. It's perfectly clear that we cannot rely on Facebook to police their own system; to be fair to them, the sheer amount of data published on the site every day makes it next to impossible, so we all have to take a level of responsibility in doing it ourselves. Furthermore, the more we as librarians and information professionals can be seen to be proactive, the more we are able to promote our own profession, and also any library-related Facebook pages that we maintain.

Twitter

As mentioned earlier in the chapter, Twitter is also not immune to the spread of inaccurate information. Simply because a large number of people tweet or retweet something doesn't mean that it's accurate, so it's necessary to double- or even triple-check your sources before using material that you find there.

The first thing to do is to try and track the story right back to an original tweet. If you catch a story early this may be fairly easy, since people will often just retweet the original. However, once the story has been out there for several minutes or a few hours, this is going to much more difficult. You can of course use Twitter's own search function, but unfortunately their own tool is notoriously unreliable. You may find it more sensible to use an independent search engine such as Topsy, at www.topsy.com, which indexes up to 600 million tweets per day. You can limit results to particular time periods, check tweets over a 30-day period, and see who are the key influencers for a particular subject, event or hashtag.

Another useful tool is the Wefollow directory, at www.wefollow.com, which claims that you can 'discover prominent people'. Wefollow gives you the opportunity to search by interest and the resource will give you a list of people who match that particular interest, arranged by 'prominence score'. Alternatively, using the SocialMention* search engine (please note that the asterisk is part of the name!), at www.socialmention.com, will also identify top users who are tweeting about a particular subject.

Klout, at http://klout.com, is also worth checking when assessing the authority of an individual. Simply type in the name of the person that you want to find out more about – or if you're already sure of their name a good shortcut is to just add it to the URL (e.g., http://klout.com/#/Philbradley) and Klout will pull up their content from Twitter, but also other social media platforms as well. Klout also assigns everyone a Klout score, and the closer to 100, the more influential and important they are supposed to be. However, since pop stars do have a tendency to reach close to the magical 100, it's something that is worth taking with a large pinch of salt, though I suppose comparing people like for like may be a little more illuminating.

Once you have located particular individuals who have some close association with the story that you are investigating, check out their profile. How long have they been active on Twitter? How many tweets have they posted? How many followers do they have, and how many people are they following themselves? While the former choice may seem to be sensible, it's actually not a very useful metric. It's very easy to purchase Twitter followers; there's a really large trade in this. Prices do vary, but I have seen advertisements that offer 5000 Twitter followers for the knockdown price of US$5. Sadly, people are sometimes tempted by this ploy, in the hope that it will make them seem more important than they really are. If you have any doubts about a person, and want to see if some of their followers are fake, there are a number of tools that you can use, such as StatusPeople Fake Followers at http://fakers.statuspeople.com. Perhaps a more useful metric is to find out if they are on any lists that other Twitter users have compiled, and if so, what are they? Have they linked to a particular website? If they have, visit that as well. If the person involved is particularly well known, or is a celebrity figure, has their account been verified by Twitter? If it has, it should have a tick next to the name.

Once you have checked out all of these points you should have a very clear indication of the extent to which you can trust the story that you're researching. You can then move on to the next step, which is checking it against other news sources. However, sometimes this may not be possible: if the story is a breaking one, traditional news sites may not yet have picked up on it, or the story may be very local and of no interest to the national press, or it may be a niche subject area. In that case, it's going to be necessary to check with your own authoritative sources, perhaps on Twitter, perhaps not. In any case, once you are satisfied, you may wish to tweet yourself, to add weight to the story or to help debunk it. The more that we as a profession can be seen as checking authority and validity, the more we can be trusted, both as a group, and as individuals.

LinkedIn

The LinkedIn site, at www.linkedin.com is another website that can be used to check the authority and validity of a particular individual. Most people are well aware of LinkedIn, but if you're not, it's a directory of over 250 million professionals, who can make their CV or resumé available online. People can connect to each other and can recommend them, or confirm their skills and expertise in different subject areas. It's helpful to be able to see information such as their career backgrounds and experience, the companies that they have worked for, their qualifications, their connections and the LinkedIn discussion groups that they have joined. The LinkedIn search function is very comprehensive, with filters for people, jobs, companies, articles, relationships, specific companies, locations, industries and so on.

As with everything else, of course, the extent to which you can trust the content that you find on LinkedIn is entirely up to you. People may well exaggerate their experience for example, and it's highly unlikely that their contacts are going to question that (at least, not publicly). The endorsement function is of very limited value, I would say from personal experience; I have been endorsed for skills that I simply don't possess and it's far too easy to simply return the favour by clicking on the collection of skills that LinkedIn assumes that someone else has. However, as an initial tool to research and check a person's authority, this is a useful resource, and, of course, if you have a contact in common you can always ask for their opinion as well.

Google properties

Google can be a useful way of checking the authority and validity of both content and the individuals who post it. Google is in competition with Facebook in the eternal fight to get eyeballs on adverts, and has introduced its own social network, Google+. When possible, Google will incorporate data from their network in the results that they display on the screen. Figure 2.1 shows an example from a search for a friend of mine, Danny Sullivan, who is one of the world's leading experts on internet search.

Google provides us with a side box of information, which gives us information that Danny is included in over 1,740,000 Google+ circles. That denotes the number of people who follow what Danny does, and want to be kept up to date about what he says and posts. On the right-hand side we

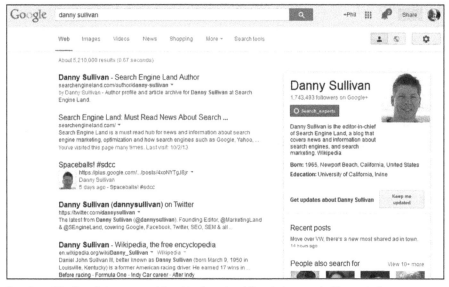

Google and the Google logo are registered trademarks of Google Inc., used with permission

Figure 2.1 Screenshot of a Google result for Danny Sullivan

can see photographs of people with the same name, but there is also a brief profile of Danny, details of his latest post, and links to people who are similar to him and have also been the subject of searches. It's a comprehensive, albeit short, round-up of Danny, and if I didn't know him, it would give me a lot of confidence that he is an authority in his field.

A person's YouTube channel can also be quite illuminating – you can see what they have posted, how many views they have had, comments on their videos, what they have liked themselves and so on.

I can go much further than this, since I can actually go into Google+ and run a search for the person who interests me. Google will show me appropriate matches and I can choose the one that is my match. It's then simply a question of checking through their profile, seeing the things that they post, responses to posts they have made and see the number of Google+ +1s (similar to Facebook 'likes') the posts have. I can also see the number of views that the profile has had, which is also helpful. You can see an example of this by looking at my profile at https://plus.google.com/+PhilBradleyUK, as illustrated in Figure 2.2.

Moreover, by clicking on the 'About' link, Google+ provides even more information, as supplied by the individual concerned. Interested parties will be able to see people who are in my Google+ circles, people who have

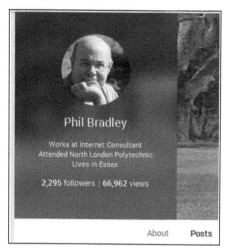

Figure 2.2
The author's Google+ profile

me in theirs, basic information about me and links to my other profiles. This is a very helpful section, as it allows people to immediately click through to check out my blogs, Flickr account, Twitter presence, my YouTube channel, and so on. Now, while it is possible to create an entirely fake persona on Twitter or Facebook for example, it's more difficult to do the same thing within the Google environment, because Google links so many different aspects of your online life together. I'm not saying that it's impossible to create fake accounts, but it's more time-consuming to do it really well. Consequently, checking the validity or authority of a person is reasonably straightforward within the Google environment. While Google doesn't as yet use any particular system of author ranking, despite the moves that I've mentioned above, it does seem very likely that they will move in this direction in the future. Matt Cutts, a senior member of Google staff, said in 2013:

> We're doing a better job of detecting when someone is more of an authority on a specific space. You know, it could be medical. It could be travel. Whatever. And try to make sure that those rank a little more highly if you're some sort of authority or a site, according to the algorithms, we think might be a little more appropriate for users.
>
> www.webpronews.com/google-says-its-now-working-to-promote-good-guys-2013-12

Blogs

Blogs have been around since before the turn of the century, and they are an established way of providing content to readers. This may simply be in the form of a personal diary, or it may be rather more involved and professional than that – an expert finding good-quality content, linking to it and then discussing it. The main drawback with blogs is that the writer will always have an opinion on what they choose to write about (and equally what they choose not to write about), so while blogs can be a good way to check the authority of the content that you're researching they do need to be used with care.

Obviously it's perfectly possible to use the tools mentioned in this chapter to research the author, but it's just as interesting to research the blog itself. A good starting point can be Google's Blogsearch engine, at www.google.com/blogsearch, which will find and display appropriate blogs that match the subject area of the search. Google provides a small listing at the start of the search results titled 'Blog homepages for <subject>' and this is always a good starting point to see who is writing on a particular subject. Technorati, at www.technorati.com is getting a little long in the tooth now, but you can still use it to search for blogs, and it provides a useful filter for authority: high, medium or low. Alltop, at http://alltop.com, has, its name suggests, a reputation for providing tightly grouped blog lists of the most informative sites available.

The news search engine Silobreaker, at http://news.silobreaker.com, also links through to blogs that mention the subject that is being searched for, and this can be really helpful in narrowing down content to blogs that contain information in the news.

When assessing a blog it's necessary to see how long it has been publishing, any details on the author(s), the number and type of comments, how focused on a subject it is, transparency (does the blogger make it clear if he/she blogs for some reward?). How sophisticated is its use of language and spelling? Is the blogger responding to a story as it is breaking, or is it a retrospective posting? It doesn't really matter these days which blogging platform someone uses, although well known ones are Blogger, WordPress and Typepad at www.blogger.com, www.wordpress.com and www.typepad.com respectively; they're just the tools that someone chooses to use because they like the style of a particular package, ease of use, free templates and so on.

Other ways to check authority

The ease with which people can create content is a double-edged sword. As we have seen, setting up fake pages on Facebook is simple, and so is having a large number of Twitter followers. While I'm not going to suggest that we are all active on social media (some of us do have jobs to do, after all), it's worth checking a variety of other sites to find experts, and to check out the content that you find. Slideshare, at www.slideshare.net, and AuthorStream, at www.authorstream.com, are both good sites to identify experts in particular subject areas, but as you are no doubt coming to expect now, you need to check out the profile of the authors of the presentations. How many followers do they have, and where are they from? How many presentations do they have available for people to look at, and how many people have looked at them? Do they allow people to comment, embed or download the presentations? – while there is nothing wrong if they don't, it's something that you may find influencing your opinion.

Another key social network that is worth checking out is Pinterest, at www.pinterest.com (see page 133). While the basic concept of the site is simple – bookmarking images from web pages – there is much more to it than that. Searchers can look for specific subjects or particular individuals, and can then check to see how many followers someone has, how often the images that they have pinned have been repinned and if they are members of specific groups or folders, sharing content with other people.

The SEO Review Tools site, at www.seoreviewtools.com/social-authority-checker, has released a 'social page authority checker' that ranks websites by their social interactions; Google+ counts, Twitter shares, total Facebook likes and shares, LinkedIn share counts and also Pinterest pins. The higher the calculated social media interaction, the higher the social media authority score for a specific URL. Essentially it's checking to see how visitors interact and like the content on the site. Of course, this could be manipulated by someone who wished to be underhand, but I think it's fair to say that this would require much more work than simply altering the rank of a page in a traditional search engine.

Summary

The strength and weakness of social media content comes from the people who produce it. It's not always clear if a tweet has come from an expert in their field, or is simply an opinion voiced by a child. Facebook doesn't monitor pages or posts for accuracy, and YouTube has 100 hours of video content uploaded every minute.

The plain fact of the matter is that content cannot be trusted; at least not in the way that we used to be able to trust content, because that would go through a publishing house or magazine or would be subject to peer reviews and citations. It's up to everyone to attempt to police social media themselves now; if you see something offensive on YouTube you can report it, and you can do the same on Facebook or report a spammer on Twitter – but this is really just for people or posts that are unpleasant, contain hate speech or break the law, for example. None of these tools are going to remove material just because it's inaccurate, and indeed who are they to say that it is? A person who believes that the moon landings never occurred has every right to express their viewpoint – it's up to the rest of us to decide on the accuracy or validity of that viewpoint.

We're really starting to see that social media content is changing the way in which we view material – of course web pages are still important, and they will continue to be important well into the future. However, because so much information is now being produced which does not go through any kind of web editing process, or which has to meet the requirements of the person or organization posting it, more content is available via other sources. A tweet can be as authoritative as a web page; it depends on who tweeted what. We are beginning to see the importance of the individual more than ever before. If I'm searching for an expert in an area I'll certainly look to see which university they come from (if they do!), but that's now only one of the many ways in which I can work out for myself their level of credibility. As we've seen in this chapter there are plenty of tools that can be used – though probably none as useful as common sense – but once we have found our experts, or good and credible websites, what can we do next?

One of the roles that is going to be increasingly important in the future is our ability to take the information that we have gathered, repackage it and then make it available to other people. People trust information professionals, and we can leverage that trust by becoming beacons pointing to good-quality information, irrespective of its origin, but because so much of it comes from the social media environment, that's perhaps where we need to focus our attention. In the next chapter I'll look at some of the ways in which we can provide our members with the guiding tools that will help them find the information that they need.

URLs mentioned in this chapter

Alltop http://alltop.com

AuthorStream www.authorstream.com
Blogger www.blogger.com
Dihydrogen Monoxide Research Division www.dhmo.org
Dog Island www.thedogisland.com
Google's Blogsearch engine www.google.com/blogsearch
Google+ (author's profile) https://plus.google.com/+PhilBradleyUK
Hoax-Slayer www.hoax-slayer.com
Klout http://klout.com
LinkedIn www.linkedin.com
Pinterest www.pinterest.com
SEO Review Tools www.seoreviewtools.com/social-authority-checker
Silobreaker http://news.silobreaker.com
Slideshare www.slideshare.net
Snopes www.snopes.com
SocialMention* www.socialmention.com
StatusPeople Fake Followers http://fakers.statuspeople.com
Technorati www.technorati.com
Topsy www.topsy.com
Typepad www.typepad.com
Wefollow www.wefollow.com
Wordpress www.wordpress.com

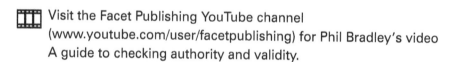 Visit the Facet Publishing YouTube channel
(www.youtube.com/user/facetpublishing) for Phil Bradley's video
A guide to checking authority and validity.

CHAPTER 3

Guiding tools

Introduction

There's nothing new about guiding users; it's something that information professionals do all of the time. We choose the titles to purchase, the databases to subscribe to, the magazines to display. Of course, we're not telling them what they should do with the information that they find, but we're acting as a reliable source or beacon to help them on their way.

In the age of the internet we have simply moved from one way of guiding to another – most library or information sites will have lists of useful websites or web pages that users may find helpful when they are doing their own research. While it is helpful, it's very difficult to make such a list interesting or attractive for people to use. When faced with a long and, let's face it, boring list of URLs it takes someone with a strong heart or desperation to actually go through the list looking for what they need. These lists are also quickly out of date, content changes, and they need to be refreshed manually. It can also be quite difficult to share these helpful lists with other people, without requiring them to constantly return to your own website.

With the increase in social media tools however, the ability to provide guiding for library members has exploded. We can set up start or home pages that come up immediately a browser is activated, we can pull in RSS or newsfeeds to keep up to date with what is happening in a particular subject area, or we can make our own search engines for members to use. Alternatively, when we find information ourselves (either by searching directly for it or serendipitously) we can quickly share this with people in a variety of different ways.

In this chapter I shall look at some of the tools that the library can use; easy to establish, quick and simple to maintain, attractive to look at and costing nothing except some time.

Home or start pages

When we open up our browsers, it's usually because we want to do something – check our e-mail, see what current affairs are occurring, run a search, keep up to date with blogs, do a currency conversion and so on. Unfortunately for most of us, the page that the browser opens up – the home or start page (either term can be used, though home page is more common, but they both mean the same thing) is seldom the one that is going to be particularly helpful. It might be the page for the library service, for the university or college or for the local council, or it may open onto a search engine. In any event, it's probably not terribly helpful. Home pages allow people to create a different type of page, one that's dynamic, interesting and full of useful information, and it may well answer a person's query there and then.

A reasonably simple example is Symbaloo, at www.symbaloo.com. It is based on the idea of creating tiles, and when users click on a tile they get taken to the corresponding page. Figure 3.1 shows my home page.

Used with permission from Symbaloo

Figure 3.1 The author's Symbaloo home page

I have this page set to appear on my desktop (when I'm using Firefox) and my laptop, and it can also be used with my tablet and smartphone. It's essentially my own portal to the entire internet. My page links to various search engines, websites that I regularly visit, some utilities that provide access to navigation facilities or percentage calculators and so on. Finally, the collection in the middle at the top with the small RSS feed in the top corner of each tile allows me to check the news whenever I wish. Figure 3.2 shows the current news headlines from around the world, as provided by the BBC.

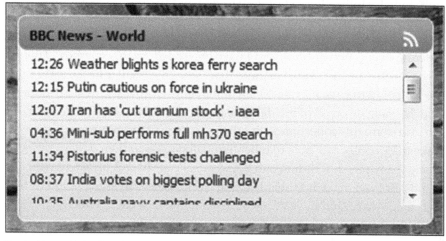

Used with permission from Symbaloo

Figure 3.2 An RSS feed pulled from the BBC News website

It's a very easy tool to use – I can simply click on an empty tile and choose to add an existing tile or create one from scratch. To use an existing Symbaloo tile I just search for a tile, such as any links to *The Guardian* newspaper itself or its RSS feeds (Figure 3.3).

I can then click on the tile that I want and immediately add it to my

Used with permission from Symbaloo

Figure 3.3
The Symbaloo tiles for 'The Guardian' newspaper

collection. Alternatively I can edit it to change the colour of the tile, the wording on it and I can choose an icon or image if I don't like the default option. If I can't find a link to the site or feed that interests me, I can just create a tile from scratch and provide the appropriate URL, then once again edit to taste by changing colours, text and icons.

A resource like this is an extremely good way to save yourself a lot of time when you're online – it's almost like having a set of bookmarks or favourites on steroids! However, while it's useful to have your own collection, it's much more helpful to be able to provide access to other people. Sharp-eyed readers will have noticed that in Figure 3.1 there are a series of tabs along the top of the webmix (the term that Symbaloo uses to describe a collection of tiles), and I have one called 'Search engines'. This lists over 50 different search engines that I use on a regular basis, and I find it very handy to have it available all of the time. Of course, since my home page is available on all of my devices, I'm never without them. However, I can also share this collection with other people via the 'share' tab. I can make the webmix available to other Symbaloo users in their gallery by giving it a name, description and keywords, I can share it privately with friends, or I can make it available to the world to use. So if you're interested, you can go along and have a look yourself at the collection, which is available at www.symbaloo.com/mix/searchengines34. You don't need to have an account to look at the page either, though if you do, you can add it to your own collection.

It's therefore a great tool to enable you to share content with your users. You can create a home page that automatically starts with the browser. It can link to all of the pages that you feel your users may be interested in from your organization rather than having to rely on a single home page, and you can also create other tabs for different subject areas. If you have a local history group in the community, for example, you could set up a tab that covers exactly that, with lots of links to useful sites. Not only can people copy these and amend their own copy to accurately reflect their own interests (without changing your original), but you can have as many different tabs set up as you need. You are not limited to the number of tiles that you see on the screen either – the page can be edited to increase the columns or rows and add your own background as well, to give it a slightly more corporate feeling.

If Symbaloo isn't to your taste there are plenty of other straightforward home pages, such as Startme, at www.startme.com, Trackpanel, at https://trackpanel.net, or YourPort, at www.yourport.com.

However, there are more complex options available to you, and a good example of this is Netvibes, at www.netvibes.com. This tool uses small 'widgets' to create data for you. For example, you can create a widget to visit news sites actively and bring back content for you, provide you with a multiple search box for different search engines, keep a collection of bookmarks, keep tabs on sites such as Delicious, run and continually update 'canned' searches for you, create notes on a Netvibes page into the 'notebook widget', pull in photographs from Flickr, provide you with an option of posting directly to a Twitter account and much more. In fact there are many thousands of different widgets that can be configured for use with an account. As with Symbaloo, tabs are private by default, but they can be made available for other people to share. My public Netvibes page is at www.netvibes.com/philbradley and it links into my own website, photographs, weblog postings, presentations and videos, as well as many other 'widgets'. Consequently, it's a really nice way to gather together different aspects of my social media life, but more importantly it's a good way for a library or information centre to display its activities in one place. Links to the website, Twitter feeds, Facebook status updates, photographs and video channels, for example, are all in one handy screen. Moreover, it's possible to make many other tabs available for users, so if the library has a particular specialism, or wants to make a certain subject available to members, Netvibes is a good potential option. It's widely used by library services already, with Dublin City Public Libraries, at www.netvibes.com/dublincitypubliclibraries#Home being a good example. Their Netvibes pages link to blog posts, their social networks, links to searching the catalogue, renewing books online, finding out what the local council is doing, access to subscription databases (although only if you're a member!), and recommended reads, for example. That's also just the general page – there are tabs for News, Entertainment, the European Press, Traffic and Travel, a Media Zone and Child and Teenagers Zones. Another example is that of the University of Sheffield University Library, at www.netvibes.com/universityofsheffieldlibrary#Home, which has tabs for World News, Open Access, Table of Contents and so on.

So Netvibes is a powerful tool that librarians can use in various different ways. It allows them to pull all of their disparate activities together in one place to better and more easily promote them, it can link out to other related sites or pull in data that will be of interest to the members of the library. Also of particular value is the fact that RSS feeds and canned searches are updated on a regular (usually hourly) basis, so once the Netvibes widgets and pages have been set up they need next to no maintenance, while retaining a high level of functionality.

As you would expect, there are plenty of other tools that are very similar to Netvibes, so if for some reason you don't like their offering try out BlueG, at www.blueg.com/personal, Dash, at https://www.thedash.com, or UStart, at www.ustart.org.

Pearltrees

Unusually for social media-based tools, Pearltrees has no competition at all. I generally find that if a tool is particularly helpful then look-alike resources will quickly appear. However, in this instance Pearltrees is so different I doubt that it would be possible to make something similar without it being a direct copy. The idea behind Pearltrees is to allow the creator of the content to link various websites, pages, images or files together in a semi-hierarchical format. Users can click on a 'Pearltree' to enter it, then click on a subject heading and then click to see individual collections of links and content. Since it sounds rather more complicated than it is, it's best to show how this works visually. You can visit my collection of Pearltrees, at www.pearltrees.com/philbradley and you'll see something similar to that shown in Figure 3.4.

You can see that I have a number of 'Pearltrees' leading off from my

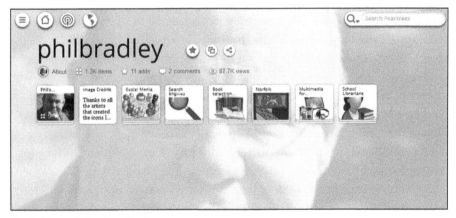

Used with permission from Pearltrees

Figure 3.4 The author's Pearltree collection

central point, such as 'Multimedia for Librarians', 'Social Media' and 'Search Engines'. If I click on the Search Engines option, this then opens out into the screen, providing the user with various further options (Figure 3.5).

Used with permission from Pearltrees

Figure 3.5 The Search Engines Pearltree

I can then click onto another link, such as 'Social Media search', and then get access to resources in that category, as can be seen in Figure 3.6.

Used with permission from Pearltrees

Figure 3.6 Social Media search engines on Pearltrees

The searcher can then click on anything that is of particular interest and see a little more information on the web page or resource before clicking on it to leave Pearltrees behind and go and visit it.

Pearltrees is a very visual tool, and is very graceful, as each tree expands or contracts. It will attempt to take a screenshot of the page that is being linked to and will use that as the icon, but you can upload your own if you prefer to make it visually more appealing. New Pearltrees can quickly be added or copied as needed, so it's easy to copy what has already been created elsewhere without having to redo an entire tree. Individual pearls can be moved around in order, or attached to existing pearls. This allows the creation of a Pearltree with many hundreds of links if necessary.

It's possible to link different trees together, so you can quickly collaborate with someone else who is working in the same area that you are, or you can allow other people to curate your Pearltrees as well. This gives librarians a real opportunity to work independently of each other, but also to collaborate and create an entire collection (dare I call it a web?) of Pearltrees, all interconnected, but each having a different focus. The trees can also be embedded onto a blog or a website, which allows for integration into an existing internet presence. It should also be noted that it's very easy to create a Pearltree and creators need only add in the URL of the web page that they want to link to, then click and drag the resulting pearl wherever they want it to go. It is, therefore, a superb tool for library and information professionals to use. Having created a collection of high-quality sites and links it would be a shame not to make as much use of them as possible, and Pearltrees provides users with an opportunity to do exactly that.

Google customized search engines

One of the problems that you find when searching the internet is that the search engine returns a lot of rubbish. Neil Gaiman's famous quote really says all that needs saying; 'Google can bring you back 100,000 answers. A librarian can bring you back the right one.' While I would never want to contradict him, and agree entirely with what he says, it's so much better if the librarian can work in conjunction with Google. If you have a collection of web pages or websites that are made available for users, how much more useful would it be to be able to just search those specific resources, rather than everything else?

This is where the Google customized search engines come into play. In order to create a personalized search engine it's first of all necessary to have your own Google account, which should come as no surprise. Once you have your own account you can visit the customizing page at https://www.google.com/cse. It's at this point you can create your own engine. Simply give it a name, add in the URLs of the sites, folders or web pages that you would like to include in the search operation, give it a description and keywords then let Google create it for you.

Once the engine is created Google will host it for you on their own site and will also provide the embedded code that you can use to add it to other places, such as a home or start page, blog or website. Users can then use the engine in exactly the same way that they have always done in the past, using the normal Google search functionality, and will be given a set of results, as usual. The only difference is that the results will only be pulled from the sites you have specified, rather than from across the entire web. This way you can guarantee the quality and authority of the results while not interfering with the users' searches.

Bookmarking packages

A slightly different approach to making content available for users is to use one of the many tools that allow people to save their bookmarks (or 'favourites', depending on the browser being used) into the cloud, where they can be shared with other people. There are many tools available: I just want to focus on a couple of them to show how they work, and how they can best be used. In general terms the concept is very straightforward. Browsers have inbuilt functionality to allow users to bookmark specific web pages that are of interest to them, and these can be arranged into folders for easy retrieval. It makes life much easier when browsing around the web to find a useful page and then make a note of it so that you can come back to it later. However, there are disadvantages to this approach – first, it only works on a single computer (unless you are using something like Xmarks, at www.xmarks.com, which allows users to sync bookmarks across browsers and machines), and it's not easy to share them with anyone else. The bookmark option on the browser is therefore very limited. However, a bookmarking tool takes the basic concept and expands it – by clicking on a 'bookmarklet' that is added to the browser. The page that's of interest is stored externally in the cloud, where it can easily be retrieved but can also be shared with other people or used in other ways, e.g. by copying the bookmarks elsewhere, such as onto a web page, automatically.

Delicious

The bookmarking site Delicious, at www.delicious.com, was founded in 2003 and by the time it was sold to AVOS Systems in 2011 had over 5 million users, who had bookmarked 180 million unique URLs. It did go through a rather difficult period as the new owners took it back to basics, but it's still a widely used system and worth some consideration. As described above, it's very easy to use – install the bookmarklet onto your browser (this is done automatically for you) and when you find a page that you want to add to your collection, simply click on the link or icon. Delicious will then open up a dialogue box for you with the URL and title of the page automatically added, and you can then add any tags you wish to help you define the content of the page. You can then add some comments about the page that you feel are appropriate, make it public or private and share it to Twitter or Facebook.

You can then visit your collection (you can see mine at https://delicious.com/philbradley) whenever necessary, using any machine that has internet access. Delicious also supports a networking or community-based approach, in that you can choose to follow other people or be followed by them, discover community-picked links based on your own interests and create your own profile for other people to learn more about you. Delicious has a search function, as you'd expect, so that it's simplicity itself to find links that you need, just by typing in an appropriate tag. This functionality extends to other users as well, so that if you wanted to see all of the bookmarks that I had added about Google you can simply type the URL https://delicious.com/philbradley/google and you'll see them all displayed for you to see – or at least those that I chose to make public (which in this case is all of them). If you want to combine terms simply add a ',' (comma) symbol to the end of the URL and add in another term, such as https://delicious.com/philbradley/google,seo and the results will be limited to bookmarks that I have tagged with both terms. Delicious also allows users to create 'tag bundles' which is a collection of tags, usually to group similar pages together, and these can be shared with followers. Alternatively, you could always link users to a specific tag from your web page or blog. Delicious used to provide useful scripts to add 'tagrolls' to web pages, and these would display the most recent bookmarks that had been added, but unfortunately these have been discontinued, though it's worthwhile keeping an eye open to see if they reintroduce the functionality in the future. However, it is possible to make use of RSS feeds to add to other resources, such as the widgets in home or start pages, and Delicious provides more information on this at https://delicious.com/rss.

Diigo

Diigo, at https://www.diigo.com, works in exactly the same way as Delicious – a bookmarklet that you can call up at any point, add the page that you want to keep a note of, and add in any tags that you wish. These can then be kept private or shared publicly. In order to see my collection, for example, you can visit https://www.diigo.com/user/philbradley. Diigo allows you to follow other people, and to be followed by them, but it has also created a 'My groups' option, which Delicious hasn't. This allows people to discuss things of interest with other like-minded people, based around the concept of collecting tagged pages. The 'Community' option allows Diigo users to see what is 'hot' or trending at any particular moment.

Diigo naturally has a search function as well, so it's easy to see exactly what pages other people think are of particular value, and it's worth directing users to this function to discover what's really of interest to people, rather than what search engines think is appropriate. There are also other tools, such as the ability to e-mail links, publish them to a blog or to create a 'word cloud' of tags. You can also save or cross-post links to Delicious or auto-blog your bookmarks daily or weekly.

Both Delicious and Diigo allow links that are posted to Twitter to be saved automatically, which is a really helpful way of backing up what you share with your Twitter community. There's also a specific tool called Packrati.us, at http://packrati.us, which does the same thing.

It almost goes without saying that if you are not interested in either of these tools, there are plenty of others available, such as Moovlink, at http://moovlink.com, MyBookmarks, at www.mybookmarks.com, or Pinboard, at http://pinboard.in.

Blending bookmarks into a social media strategy

Hopefully you can already see ways in which you can do rather more with a collection of bookmarks than would ever be possible with a collection on a standalone computer. By combining the use of tweeted links with a bookmarking solution you can always ensure that all of the content that you think is useful and valuable can be quickly and automatically stored.

These bookmarked links are then shared via RSS to a web page or a start page, with no further input from you than initially setting the system up. You can guide your colleagues and library members by linking them to your bookmarked collection or to a subset of it, and as long as you continue to use the system your content will be continually updated.

Social bookmarking systems have several advantages over traditional search engines. All of the tagging is done by human beings (although an increasing number of systems are suggesting appropriate tags) and they understand the content and quality of the resource. Search engines, on the other hand, have to use a complex algorithm which doesn't always work correctly. A search of a bookmarked collection of pages may therefore return more appropriate and accurate results, which can sometimes be rather more trustworthy than those from the search engines.

Bookmarking systems generally offer web authors the chance to add appropriate icons to their pages, encouraging users to bookmark them, and this may well help with a long-term promotion strategy – helping people promote the site or the resource themselves without further intervention.

Summary

It's important that we don't allow ourselves to be overwhelmed by the amount of information that is flooding onto the internet every day. However, rather than look at this as a problem, it's actually a really good opportunity for the information professional to provide added value to users or library members. We can find the 'good' material (however that is defined) and make it available in new and interesting ways. We should by all means continue to provide people with straightforward access to websites and pages, just as we have always done, but equally we can now provide that same information in much more dynamic and effective ways in the future. If you have any sort of list of websites in hand-outs or presentations or on library web pages consider making them available using one of the tools mentioned in this chapter. Furthermore, save yourself time by encouraging users to view your bookmarked collection, to keep themselves right up to date with the information you find.

Of course, bookmarking and guiding is useful, but it does have its drawbacks, and this is where another type of tool comes into play for the hard-worked information professional – current awareness or selective dissemination of information resources. I'll cover these in the next chapter.

URLs mentioned in this chapter

BlueG www.blueg.com/personal

Dash https://www.thedash.com

Delicious www.delicious.com

- ▦ Author's Delicious collection https://delicious.com/philbradley
- ▦ RSS feed information https://delicious.com/rss

Diigo https://www.diigo.com

Author's Diigo collection https://www.diigo.com/user/philbradley

Google www.google.com/cse

- ▦ Google customizing search engine page

Moovlink http://moovlink.com

MyBookmarks www.mybookmarks.com

Netvibes www.netvibes.com

- ▦ Author's public Netvibes page www.netvibes.com/philbradley
- ▦ Dublin City Public Libraries Netvibes pages
  www.netvibes.com/dublincitypubliclibraries#Home
- ▦ University of Sheffield University Library Netvibes pages
  www.netvibes.com/universityofsheffieldlibrary#Home

Packrati.us http://packrati.us

Pearltrees www.pearltrees.com

- ▦ Author's collection of Pearltrees www.pearltrees.com/philbradley

Pinboard http://pinboard.in

Startme www.startme.com

Symbaloo www.symbaloo.com

- ▦ Author's search engines page
  www.symbaloo.com/mix/searchengines34

Trackpanel https://trackpanel.net

UStart www.ustart.org

Xmarks www.xmarks.com

YourPort www.yourport.com

▦ Visit the Facet Publishing YouTube channel
(www.youtube.com/user/facetpublishing) for Phil Bradley's video
A guide to creating pages in Symbaloo and Pearltrees.

CHAPTER 4

Current awareness and selective dissemination of information resources

Introduction

Keeping track of particular subjects or areas of interest, and then letting specific library users know about the information that you have found, is not new – it's one of the staples of being an information professional. In 'the old days' you may well have e-mailed someone when you had found something new for them, or it might have been information that was squirrelled away and put into the monthly newsletter update. Or you may have decided on a more informal approach, by catching someone when you saw them in the corridor to let them know about the next new thing that they would find interesting.

However, social media – user-generated content – is changing the way in which we let people know what we have found, or to distribute it to specific individuals according to their interests. We have already looked at a few of those in previous chapters – it's easy to create a home or start page widget with a search phrase already in it, so that a user can simply click on it to see the latest information. Alternatively, we can remind our users to look at our bookmark resource in order to find the new content. Those options are useful, of course, but there is a whole raft of other tools that allow us to take this activity to a new social media-enhanced level. Rather than simply link to a resource, tweet it or bookmark it, we are now in a position to pull in an entire story to read, or to allow others to do so. Furthermore, when it comes to finding information that's necessary for each of us to do our own jobs effectively we no longer need to go out and seek the information that we need – the content comes directly to us with very little hard work on our part.

Let the networks take the strain!

One of the questions that I am asked a lot as an internet consultant is 'How do you keep up to date?' and it's a very fair question. There is so much information flooding onto the net on a daily basis – or even on a minute-by-minute basis – that it can be hard to sort out the wheat from the chaff and just focus on the really important material. Once again harking back to the old days, it was a really difficult job. I would spend hours reading through blog posts from librarians and other experts to see what information they had found, what the key topics were and who was talking about what. I'd also run canned searches on a regular, sometimes daily basis to get new material, and I made a lot of use of 'web page watchers' which would e-mail me when certain key pages changed. In other words – I had to go out and find the information myself, it wasn't coming directly to me. In truth, this one job would take up a major part of my daily work, and for people with 'real' jobs, it simply wasn't possible. However, with the advent of social media, it's much easier to keep on top of what people are finding, because you can use your own networks to tell you exactly what's important and trending.

Twitter is an excellent tool for this. I talk about Twitter in much more detail in Chapter 7, so I'll just briefly focus on one or two elements here that are pertinent to the subject at hand. Twitter lists are an excellent tool, but widely underused. Twitter of course tells you when you're being followed by someone new, and you can then add them to any lists that you have created. If you prefer, you don't actually need to follow them back, but they can still be included in the list. It's entirely up to you as to what sort of list it is – it might be a list of people that you've met in real life, a list of school librarians, a list of favourite musicians and so on. You can see a collection of my lists at https://twitter.com/Philbradley/lists and as long as you have a Twitter account you can subscribe to any of them that interests you. Lists allow you to focus on the tweets sent out by that specific group of people, excluding everything else. Consequently if I want to see what school librarians are talking about I can simply click on my 'School libs librarians' collection and dive in. Now of course they'll be talking about a wide range of things, with the usual mix of personal and professional content, so it's not ideal, but it's one way to get a very quick sense of what is of interest to that group. The more you are able to focus on a subject area, and to choose the people who go into that list, the more valuable it will become. A tool such as Tweetdeck, at https://tweetdeck.

twitter.com, also provides extra search functionality, allowing a user to search for words or phrases within a specific list. This helps overcome the issue of irrelevant content and lets users really focus their search. Of course, if you are busy creating lists it's always worth sharing them with other people as well, so that they can share the results of the work that you've put in.

Alternatively, it's worth taking a look at tools which will pull content together for you, based on the Twitter account, such as The Tweeted Times, at http://tweetedtimes.com. It is described as 'a real time personalized newspaper generated from your Twitter account.' It's simplicity itself to create a newspaper, since the work is done for you – you simply have to register with your Twitter account credentials and The Tweeted Times will make the newspaper for you there and then. You can also share it with others as well; mine is at http://tweetedtimes.com/ #!/Philbradley, for example, and you're welcome to take a look around. Key stories will be displayed for me with summaries and links to the original full-text content, based on my friends who posted information or links, and the friends of friends. That way I can see the most important stories that the people I follow on Twitter are talking about in a matter of seconds. We can also create newspapers based on lists on particular search terms.

Tablet-based applications

Luckily I have access to a tablet device, and there is a wealth of different applications that you can use to keep up to date with things that are of interest to you. Probably the two that are most well known are Zite (www.zite.com) and Flipboard (www.flipboard.com). Although their physical appearance differs – Flipboard utilizes a page turning or flipping visual effect, Zite works with blocks of text and visual stories – they both do the same job. When creating an account you can also link to your Twitter and Facebook accounts, and the resources will then look at the stories that the people you follow are talking about or linking to. They are then able to provide you with access to the summary of the story, allowing you to then follow through and look at the story in depth from the appropriate website. You can also vote stories up and down, providing the tools with useful feedback on what interests you (and what doesn't) allowing them to tailor stories more accurately in the future. Both apps have options to search for content that is of interest to you, and sections sharing the main stories that are being discussed on social media platforms. As you would expect, you can share articles that you have enjoyed with friends, work colleagues and followers.

Unfortunately Zite doesn't have much by way of a web-based presence – it's designed to work on just a tablet or smartphone device – but Flipboard does, so even if you don't have either device you can still experience it via their 'magazine' experience. Flipboard also has a bookmarklet that allows you to add anything that you find in your own magazines. It's an easy way to create and share material – not just web pages but also reading lists, educational videos, lectures and so on. Conference attendees will find Flipboard to be invaluable; it's simple to add a conference hashtag to a collection of magazines, and Flipboard will then return all the references to the hashtag that it can find and the entire content, such as the news item or web page, is loaded and made available immediately. Librarians can produce easy-to-read magazines for their communities and members to keep them all abreast of the content that they will find interesting. Furthermore, creators of magazines can invite others to contribute as well, enabling an entire library staff to add to a magazine. Mine is available at http://flip.it/sSF1J in case you want to get a feel for what these look like, and there's a very good overview by Sue Waters, the editor of The Edublogger (http://theedublogger.com) contained in a YouTube video at http://youtu.be/ARcLfnaNuFM.

If neither of these applications are of interest, there are plenty of others that may appeal to you. News360 (http://news360.com) is another app that learns what is of particular interest to you and will find appropriate content. Users can create accounts with personalized newsfeeds based on Twitter, Facebook or Google+. Alternatively, Trap!t (https://trap.it) accesses over 100,000 sources which can be 'trapped' and made available to subscribers.

Web-based curation tools

As previously mentioned, the days are long gone when it was necessary to find content, store the details of it, and then disseminate it at some later point. Now all that's needed is an account with an application and the ability to add a bookmarklet to your browser. That is the hard work done in about two minutes. Most of us spend a considerable amount of time searching the web for appropriate content – it may be to answer a specific query for a library member, to update our own knowledge on a subject, to keep abreast with the news or just to explore generally and allow serendipity out to play.

Scoop.it!

Sooner or later, and it will probably be sooner, you will find content that you want to share with people, or simply to store in your own archive. There are – as you are by now expecting me to say – many tools that will do exactly that for you, but I'll just look at two or three of them in detail. The first is called Scoop.it!, at www.scoop.it. Once again, this works with something akin to a magazine format, as the screenshot in Figure 4.1 shows.

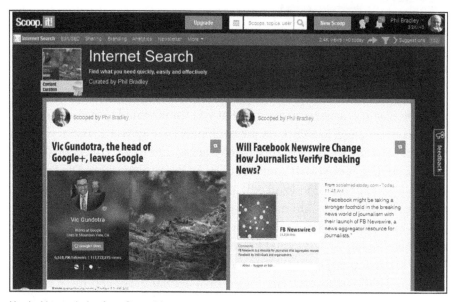

Used with permission from Scoop.it!

Figure 4.1 A screenshot from the author's Scoop.it! page

As you can see, this is from a Scoop.it! page that I curate on Internet Search, and you can find it, at www.scoop.it/t/internet-search.

In order to use Scoop.it! to curate content you need to create an account, and then decide what subject you want to focus on. You can then add the bookmarklet to your browser and carry on as normal. When you find a

Used with permission from Scoop.it!

Figure 4.2 The Scoop.it! bookmarklet in action

news item, story or website or page that you think would be a good fit for
your Scoop.it! page, just click on the bookmarklet. Figure 4.2 shows you this
in action. Having found the story that I want to add to my collection (in this
case it's about a new search engine) I click on the bookmarklet. The
dialogue box appears and I can edit all of the content that you can see, but
most particularly I can add my own insight about the story. I can then
choose to share this with my followers on different social media platforms
and when I'm happy with what I have done I can publish it, both to my
Internet Search page, and also to my other social media accounts.

Scoop.it! also suggests stories for me on a regular basis, and these will be
based on the keywords and sources that I have told it to use. I can therefore
easily tailor the content that I see and share until I am totally satisfied with
the type of suggestions the tool makes for me.

There is a search option available which allows users to find curated
topics of interest to them, and these can then be followed. The really
important point here is that everyone who curates a subject is doing so
because they are interested in it, it's within their area of expertise and they
are able to add their own insights. The message here is clear: why would
anyone want to spend – or perhaps more accurately waste – a lot of their

time trying to find good-quality content when someone else is able to do it for them? For example, I am very interested in e-books and libraries, most particularly in the UK, but I don't have the time to chase down news, see what other people are doing or generally keep up to date with the subject. Luckily, however, I don't need to, since a colleague, Alyson Tyler, is even more interested in the subject than I am, and she has created her own Scoop.it! page, at www.scoop.it/t/e-books-and-libraries which she keeps up to date. I can therefore get on with the rest of my work safe in the knowledge that Alyson is keeping me up to date, and when I need to know anything new in the area, her Scoop.it! page is the first place that I visit.

You might wonder why someone would go to the trouble of putting this content together and making it available for other people when they seemingly get little in return. I asked Alyson this question and she said 'I decided to curate a Scoop.it! page because there were too many news stories about e-books to keep up with and to share on my blog. My blog was in danger of becoming just about e-books. With the Scoop.it! page I can keep all the e-book stories in one place. I set keywords for Scoop.it! to find me relevant stories and I've actually picked up quite a few important other news stories as a result of what is in the suggested feed each day!'

There are several other reasons – it's a 'good thing to do', it makes life easier for our own colleagues and users while at the same time providing information for other people at no extra cost to the person curating the topic. However, it's also a good way to promote either yourself as an expert in a subject area, the organization that you work for, or the subject that is your own particular passion or interest. It's another example that we are now starting to move away from the idea that information is provided by corporate entities or news websites, and can instead be provided by anyone with a passion. It's also particularly appropriate for librarians, because this is what we do all of the time anyway – it's often our role to keep people informed and up to date, and using a tool such as this just makes that task so much easier to perform more effectively.

Paper.li

If for some reason you don't find that Scoop.it! matches your particular needs, an alternative resource is Paper.li, at https://paper.li. It describes itself as 'the easiest way to collect, publish and share content on the web' and it works on the idea of a daily newspaper. Its platform gives creators access to over 250 million social media posts a day and extracts and analyses over 25 million articles. Users can select their sources from places such as Twitter, Facebook, Google+, YouTube and RSS feeds. They can then define the frequency of updates, topics that should be covered and the language that's appropriate. The newspaper can then be promoted via the usual social media channels and across all devices such as desktops, tablets and smartphones. Readers can subscribe to the newspaper, and receive an e-mail notification of every new edition. The editor can add his or her own insights, automatically send out tweets to followers whenever a new edition is made available, embed the paper in an existing web page, customize backgrounds and track usage statistics. You can see the headlines from 'The Phil Bradley Daily' at https://paper.li/Philbradley#!headlines and I've provided a screenshot in Figure 4.3. Readers can simply scan through the stories and then click on any that are of particular interest to them, and can then be transported directly to the original web page. What's also important to notice is the collection of tabs under the title – headlines, photos, videos

Figure 4.3 The Paper.li newspaper, 'The Phil Bradley Daily'

and so on. This provides me with a really quick and simple way to keep up to date with what the people that I'm following are interested in, referencing and discussing.

The value of the tool should be clear, and it's very similar to that of

Scoop.it! – it allows people to quickly create professional-looking collections of documents and to display them in an attractive and easy to use format. The collection(s) can be promoted both online and offline, making it easy for interested parties to keep up to date with the latest in a particular field. For the information professional they can disseminate information and provide current awareness with a click of a mouse whenever they find anything; there is no need to be dictated to by a rigid newsletter publishing cycle, for example.

Learnist

If neither of those tools attract you, then take a look at Learnist (https://learni.st). In common with the other tools you can create a board on any topic that interests you, then curate it by adding links and information from videos, blogs, books, documents, images or, indeed, anything else on the web. The emphasis is on learning something, and your role as creator is primarily to provide content that other people will find helpful in coming to grips with a topic, but in actuality you can, of course, use the resource however you want to. You can follow other Learnist users and like, share and comment on their boards in turn. As you would expect, there's also a bookmarklet available for your browser to make the whole process even easier.

Swayy

Swayy (www.swayy.co) is a new entrant into the whole curation arena. They say of themselves that theirs is a 'personalized content discovery platform that helps you discover the most engaging content to share with your audience across social networks'. It's a free tool, but it does have various pricing plans depending on the extent to which you want to use it. However, at the free level it's still very powerful. You can add in links to your Twitter, Facebook and LinkedIn accounts and Swayy will automatically look through them and pull out topic matches. You can also add in your own topics as well, and delete any that you don't feel are appropriate.

Swayy then suggests content for you based on the topics that you have selected in a magazine-style format. You can then scroll through the news results and read them as appropriate and share to any of the social media platforms that you have connected to your account. The selection of stories is on the whole extremely accurate, and while it doesn't replace other curation tools it's certainly a very good addition to the collection.

News curation by e-mail

If you are not interested in such sophisticated tools you may prefer something much simpler and there are plenty of resources that fit the bill for you. Curate Me, at www.curate.me, is one such example: it gets the news that you're interested in directly to your e-mail inbox. You can select subjects that interest you, pull in content from your social networks and get content from various other news sources as well. Curate Me can then be fine-tuned to provide as little or as much content as you wish from each of the subject areas and you'll receive a daily e-mail with 10–12 links from the topics that you have selected. If you prefer, the briefs can be viewed in the browser as well as via e-mail, and so can be shared with a wider audience. You can find my daily brief, at www.curate.me/daily_briefs/6684071 should you be so inclined to have a look.

News.me, at www.news.me, also works primarily by e-mail as well. Simply create a free account and provide some details of the social media networks that you're active on. News.me will then find your top stories as shared by your friends. It will then send you a daily e-mail with the top five stories, and they're also available on the web, and you can make these public or private according to your wishes. Mine is at www.news.me/Philbradley if you want to see what a daily update looks like. You can only view the top 15 stories however, so it has limited flexibility, but if you're in a hurry this might be all that you need.

Summary

If your head is reeling at this point I don't blame you in the slightest. There are plenty of choices available, and they all seem to do either the same job, or very similar ones. I really can't tell you which one is the 'best' of all of them, since it's going to depend entirely on your own circumstances, what you want to do and what devices you have at your disposal. However, I'd suggest that it's worth taking a look at all of them, even if only briefly, to see if there are one or two that really attract you. Sign up and try them out for a couple of weeks; they're all free (though they may have commercial options) and they won't mind if you decide to close your account or simply walk away from it.

Once you find something that does appeal, though, you're going to need to remember to use it – that's the first problem! It's far too easy to sign up to a lot of these tools, explore them for a couple of days and then forget that they're there. Perhaps create a bookmark folder on your own browser with the bookmarklets in them, or just have one or two in your bookmarks toolbar. Make a point of alerting your social media followers when you do add something, and in all probability you'll get that retweeted or commented on in Facebook and the resulting conversation, or even just the recognition that you provided useful content, may be just the spur that you need to keep going.

Of course, with some of these tools you don't actually have to do anything at all once you have set it up – as long as you have Twitter followers or Facebook friends posting material. The resources will continue to gather together top stories and post them automatically, and as long as you have told people about the collection and linked to it, that's all that you need do. They will keep churning out good-quality material even when you're on holiday.

These news curation and current awareness tools do fit into a good niche, so it's worth blending them into your social media presence. Tweets are all well and good, but 140 characters is after all only 140 characters. By the time you have linked to some content and produced an abbreviated comment regarding it, that's the tweet filled up. A blog, on the other hand, does require rather more commitment and you really do need to consider the subject or story in some detail and then craft a post to do it and yourself justice. If you have a busy job (and who doesn't?) it's simply not feasible to do this every time you find useful material. However, the middle course is to use one or other of these tools. You're keeping people informed, creating an archive of good material, sharing it across your social media platforms and spending virtually no time doing it; an almost perfect solution.

The wider and larger your social network, the better these tools will work. If you're only following half a dozen people on Twitter or Facebook, you're not giving these resources very much to work with. However, once you start to follow hundreds, or even thousands, of people they'll be linking to and discussing stories and news items, and this gives the tools something to work with. They can then really start to work out that a particular story is valuable because dozens of your contacts start to talk about or refer to a story or link. Don't worry about the size of your social network; far too many people panic and think that they'll never be able to keep up with all of the tweets or Facebook postings. The knack is to recognize from the outset that you never will be able to keep up; that's not the point. The point is that you get a large group or collection of friends, colleagues and experts who are pooling their thoughts, links, ideas and opinions, and you can simply use a tool to jump in whenever you need to and fish out the key information when you need it. The larger and deeper the pool the more varied it is and the more valuable it becomes.

Of course, if you're looking to promote what you or your information service or library is doing these tools will also work for you; you are acting as an expert, curating content for people to use. They will remember this, and will come back to you time and time again, and if they don't, you can always remind them by sharing what you have found via your social networking platforms. Embed your content in different places, link to it and blend your resources together to provide a richer and more varied internet presence. It will pay dividends in so many different ways.

URLs mentioned in this chapter

Curate Me www.curate.me
- Author's daily brief at Curate Me www.curate.me/daily_briefs/6684071

The Edublogger http://theedublogger.com

Flipboard www.flipboard.com
- Author's magazine at Flipboard http://flip.it/sSF1J

Learnist https://learni.st

News.me www.news.me
- Author's daily update on News.me www.news.me/Philbradley

News360 http://news360.com

Paper.li https://paper.li
- 'The Phil Bradley Daily' at Paper.li https://paper.li/Philbradley#!headlines

Scoop.it! www.scoop.it
- Alyson Tyler page www.scoop.it/t/e-books-and-libraries
- Page curated by author www.scoop.it/t/internet-search

Swayy www.swayy.co

■   Overview by Sue Waters http://youtu.be/ARcLfnaNuFM
Trap!t https://trap.it
Tweetdeck https://tweetdeck.twitter.com
The Tweeted Times http://tweetedtimes.com
■   Author's newspaper http://tweetedtimes.com/#!/Philbradley
Twitter lists
■   Author's Twitter list https://twitter.com/Philbradley/lists
Zite www.zite.com

▦ Visit the Facet Publishing YouTube channel
(www.youtube.com/user/facetpublishing) for Phil Bradley's video
A Scoop.it! guide and a look at other tools for curating content.

CHAPTER 5

Presentation tools

Introduction

We've all heard of 'death by PowerPoint' and I expect that most of us have experienced it at one time or another. However, it really doesn't have to be that way, since there are lots of tools and guides available to help people create better slide decks. Since this isn't a book about making the most of Microsoft Office I'll assume that you can find those yourself – I'll concentrate on other tools instead.

Of course, we do need to ask ourselves the question 'Why does a librarian want to create presentations anyway?' There are plenty of answers to that question – we train and teach people, we put together presentations to promote the services that we offer, display presentations in libraries to brighten up the day or inform people about some subject or the other, and we can use them as a method of reporting back on an event. Of course, we also need to consider that we should be reaching out beyond the members of the library who actually choose to come in and visit us; we are there for all of the community, at any hour of the day or night. Consequently, if we create presentations that are available online we are continuing to provide a good service (and to do what we have always done), but are able to expand that service out, both geographically and chronologically to a global 24/7 resource.

Additions to PowerPoint

If you're not ready to cut the apron strings from PowerPoint (or you like using it, or don't have permission to use anything else) there are several tools that will help you make more of the presentation that you have already produced. Presentations are generally very 'flat' and it's difficult to add in everything that you want to; people are limited to the very basic details. Indeed, they should be really, as a good presentation supports the speaker rather than replaces her.

Knovio

However, it's possible to bring the speaker back into the presentation with a tool such as Knovio, at www.knovio.com. With this tool you can add your own video taken on your webcam or tablet (iPad only at the time of writing) and synchronize it with the slide content. Then it can be shared by e-mail or online via social media networks. Once you have a PowerPoint presentation you can upload it to the Knovio site. Next you can record your video via your webcam or tablet camera, clicking on each slide to move forward as you do. Once you have finished the presentation it is then uploaded, processed and made available so that you can share it. You can see an example of one of mine at http://knov.io/1dphCv6 – it's 52 slides long and takes 40 minutes to view so unless you're particularly interested in the subject matter just watching a few minutes of it will give you the idea. Alternatively, Figure 5.1 is a screenshot.

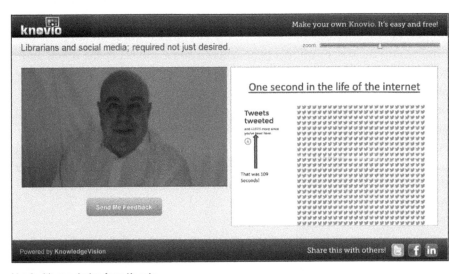

Used with permission from Knovio

Figure 5.1 A Knovio presentation by the author

You'll see in the top right-hand corner is a slider, and this allows the viewer to make the speaker's video larger than the presentation, or equal in size, or emphasize the presentation over the speaker. There is no cost to use Knovio, although they are going to introduce a premium version in the future, and they store your presentations indefinitely, so once you have recorded it, it's available from then onwards. It's useful if you have to repeatedly run the same presentation, or perhaps if you have to give a presentation somewhere and you're unable to attend in person, this is a nice way to be there virtually. If you don't like using Knovio you could try similar products such as Present.me (https://present.me) or Zentation (www.zentation.com). If you're not keen on being quite that visual you could simply narrate a presentation with Brainshark (https://www. brainshark.com) or AuthorStream (www.authorstream.com) If that still seems a little bit too personal, you could use SlideTalk, at http://slidetalk.net, which enables you to upload your presentation, type in some text for each slide; SlideTalk will convert your text into speech using one of several voices – there are five UK voices, nine US voices and many others which you can hear at http://slidetalk.net/Home/VoiceSamples.

Presentain

If you want to make your PowerPoint presentations a little more exciting, there are some options available to you. Presentain, at http://presentain. com, has both free and commercial versions available for users, and you can add polls to your presentations, view statistics real-time, and easily embed YouTube videos into slides and capture information from your audience. You can also record your presentation, then share it, increasing your audience. At the beginning of a presentation viewers are given a PIN number that they can use to log into the presentation on their device, which is how they are able to interact in the manner previously described.

Office Mix

Microsoft have introduced a product called Office Mix (https://mix.office. com). This is a tool that works with the latest version of PowerPoint (2013) and it provides an 'interactive consumption experience on devices' (Anoop Gupta, https://mix.office.com/watch/1v4koz7wvbove), as well as providing a web portal that you can use to manage, share and see the analytics for your presentations. It provides a lot of interactive features, such as high-quality animations, audio-video narration, quizzes and polls, embedded web pages and interactive simulations. Finally you can share your presentations in the cloud and view them on any device.

Participoll

Participoll, at www.participoll.com, is a free audience-polling application for PowerPoint. You can get live feedback inside existing presentations. It's free to use with unlimited live audience polling, but in order to access audience comments, historical charts and results data you need to purchase the Professional version. You can conduct as many polls as you wish and collect votes from as many audience members as you like. It's necessary to download the software to integrate it into PowerPoint, and when that's done you can simply ask the question that you want as a PowerPoint slide. Next you open the Participoll menu, choose how many answers should be available and then insert the poll into the presentation. When you reach the required point in your presentation you send your audience to the voting address that the product will give you and they can cast their votes. Everyone will then see a live count of votes received next to the results bar. When you're happy with the number of votes cast you can then move on a slide to view the results. The main disadvantages of this tool are that it's necessary to have internet connectivity available on the trainer's machine, and the audience have to be prepared to use their tablets or smartphones to connect into the internet to cast their votes.

Prezi

You may decide that you'd really like to get away from PowerPoint completely, and produce presentations in totally different formats. The good (if unsurprising) news is that there are a lot of tools available so that you can do exactly that. If you have been to any presentations or conferences recently you may find that people are presenting using a tool called Prezi, which you can find at www.prezi.com. It's quite a difficult tool to describe if you have not experienced it before, but essentially the presentation method allows you to zoom in, move around from slide to slide (although since there are no slides as such it's better to regard slides as specific segments of information), and then zoom out again. We mentioned 'death by PowerPoint'; the equivalent with Prezi is extreme travel sickness, as enthusiastic novice presenters like to cram as many features into a single presentation as they can.

However, there are plenty of excellent Prezi presentations to look at, such as the one in Figure 5.2, at http://bit.ly/socmedmusic, which is designed for music students at university, and was put together by Ned Potter, Academic Liaison Librarian at the University of York Library. I took a screenshot from several steps into the presentation, and at this point you can see an overview of what Ned is going to talk about. The Prezi then zooms into each section in turn, and moves through each information segment in turn.

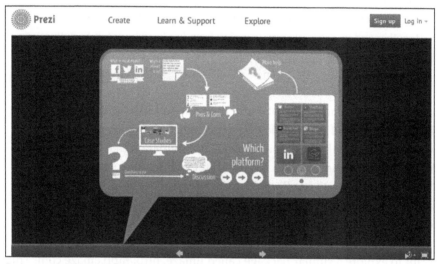

From a presentation by Ned Potter, used with permission

Figure 5.2 Prezi presentation on social media for music students

I asked Ned what his thoughts were on using Prezi, and what its strengths and weakness were. He said:

> Prezi's value to information professionals lies in its ability to help communicate complicated information in an engaging way.
>
> Although growing rapidly, Prezi is still fairly new – many or all of your audience won't have seen one before, so this freshness increases their level of engagement. I use Prezi for perhaps four out of ten presentations; it's most useful for covering several disparate topics in one talk or workshop, something which the linear nature of PowerPoint isn't suited. PowerPoint dictates the hierarchy of

information to you; you dictate the hierarchy to Prezi.

Presentations can be audience-led due to Prezi's non-linear nature (you can skip around and pick up from anywhere), and audiences find it useful to know where they are in the presentation – at the end of each section of a talk I'll zoom out so everyone can see where we've been and where we are going. It is great for innovative things like interactive maps, but you can make anything interactive – because any object you add to a Prezi will be zoomed in on when clicked. So you can annotate maps, manuscripts, diagrams. . . . It can bring analogue content to life in a way that people genuinely find exciting.

The downside is, 90% of Prezis are awful. They zoom and barrel roll around in a random order, leaving the audience disorientated and motion-sick. So use Prezi for a good reason, plan your presentation carefully, place things close together and in a sensible way (running from left-to-right or top-to-bottom), and pace the whole thing sympathetically. As long as you don't let the medium become the message, Prezi can be a hugely effective tool for communication.

It sounds like a daunting tool, but it does have a lot of advantages, as Ned has pointed out. If you are looking to provide training for your library members Prezi will allow you to create a presentation that people can dip in and out of as they need to. It's useful for training purposes and also for induction; you could use Prezi to make a map of the library and people could explore, with information segments including information on opening hours, content coverage and photographs, for example.

If you like the sound of Prezi but are uncertain about using it, you might want to explore a similar package called Emaze, http://app.emaze.com. This provides a wide variety of interesting template styles; you can make your presentation look as though it's come from a newspaper, has a 3D effect, a space theme, blossoming flowers, presentations based on the images found on an office desk, and so on. It's free to use when creating presentations from scratch, but if you want to import existing PowerPoint presentations there is a cost attached.

Interactive presentations

The tools that allow you to create a video or voiceover to accompany a presentation certainly go some way to making it more interactive, but it's still not quite there. A live presentation is, of course, more effective, and there are tools that will help to achieve that. At a very simple level you could schedule a Twitter session alongside the presentation so that people could watch it and tweet questions to you using a particular hashtag and you could respond in real time, and you could then use an application such as Storify (https://storify.com) to collect all of the tweets together and combine them into a Q&A of its own.

However, while that's not exactly clutching at straws, there are other approaches that the effective presenter can take. The Google+ Hangouts option is one that is worth considering. Google, in their quest to win long-term advantage over Facebook, introduced the social network Google+ and added in a video conferencing feature which they called a Google Hangout. It allows users to start a video conference and share thoughts and ideas back and forth, and they have added various options such as the ability to share the desktop and share presentations hosted on the Slideshare network, at www.slideshare.net. The presenter is therefore able to display the presentation, moving from slide to slide as appropriate while continuing a narrative and discussion with the other members of the Hangout. Moreover, the Hangout can be shared live across YouTube and recorded and shared across the same platform after the presentation is over.

If you are running a live presentation you may still want to add rather more excitement to it than simply moving from one tired slide to the next. Everyslide, at https://everyslide.com, allows presenters to embed instant polls directly into a presentation and add in quizzes. Indeed, if you are presenting to a group you can provide them with an Everyslide URL and they can connect directly with your presentation while you are giving it. With Projeqt (www.projeqt.com) presenters can pull in live tweets, blog feeds, interactive maps or streaming videos, all in real time. Projeqt also has what they term a 'stacks' feature, which allows you to link different presentations together so that it's possible to go off-topic, according to the interests of the participants. A similar, but leaner, tool is called Slides (http://slides.com) and this also provides presenters with the ability to move through slideshows in a non-linear format. You can upload photographs or slides and a small compass device in the bottom corner allows you to move through slides from left to right and right to left, but you can also move up or down – the best way to imagine it is to see all of your slides in a grid format that you can travel through with much more flexibility.

Timeline packages

Another type of presentation package that may appeal to information professionals is timelines. These allow creators to link content to places and periods of time. So, for example, if you were working with a group of local historians, a timeline package would assist in the creation of a presentation based on local events, people and history. An academic librarian may wish to create a timeline based around the development of a theory, while a school librarian could produce a timeline to help children better learn about a period of history and the books that would help them understand it better. Alternatively, it would be easy to create a literature map of a location, pointing to specific places and the books associated with them. Since a lot of timeline packages also allow the use of video and other multimedia it wouldn't be difficult to engage the library community in producing material themselves that could then be incorporated in a presentation.

Meograph, at www.meograph. com, is specifically designed to engage viewers by multimedia storytelling. It's very quick and simple to add in 'moments' to a presentation with an easy-to-use menu, which can be seen in Figure 5.3. This links to a presentation that I have already quickly created in about 5 minutes, and while it's not particularly exciting you can view it at http://bit.ly/1fUaAUn.

As can be seen, to create a

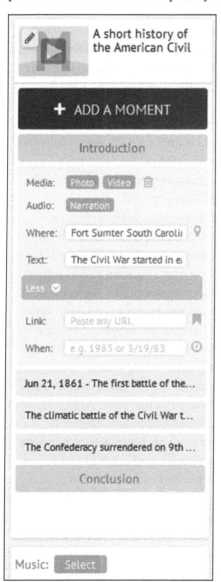

Used with permission from Meograph

Figure 5.3
The Meograph menu

multimedia presentation it's simply necessary to decide which elements you want to include – photographs, video or narrations, and if you wish to include maps and time periods those can be added in as well. When you have created one 'slide' you can then move onto the next and so on until you have created the finished article. This can then be embedded onto a website or blog, and it's also hosted on the Meograph website as well.

If you prefer something slightly different, you might wish to try Timeglider, at http://timeglider.com, which places more emphasis on specific time periods, as can be seen from the screenshot in Figure 5.4, of the history of the Wright brothers.

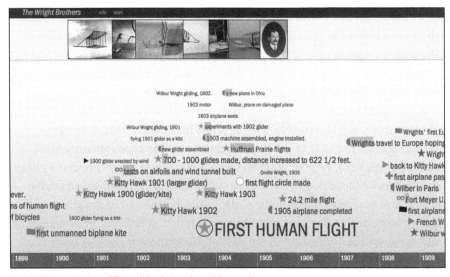

Used with permission of Timeglider (www.timeglider.com)

Figure 5.4 A Wright brothers timeline made with Timeglider

There are of course plenty of other tools available which do the same job, so you might wish to explore Dipity (www.dipity.com), Timetoast (www.timetoast.com) or Capzles (www.capzles.com).

Easy-to-create presentations

There are going to be plenty of times when you need a presentation in a hurry, or you just need something really simple to use as a backdrop for something else. This is when tools that create presentations based on images come into play. The idea is very simple; put crudely, you throw a collection of photographs at a tool and it turns it into an attractive and professionally put-together slideshow. Animoto (www.animoto.com) is a great resource for doing this. Before we talk about it, take a look at the presentation that was produced for the Umbrella Conference Finale at http://youtu.be/dNytmJXvd_s. If you are not able to view it right away, it's a collection of photographs that were taken throughout the conference mixed together with text and an exploding firework-based theme. It's very professional, but without wishing to give away many secrets, extremely easy to do. Simply upload your photographs and any video that you wish, choose from a variety of video style options, chose some appropriate text, pick a song from the Animoto library (all pre-licensed for use) and let the tool do the rest of the work. It will put the content together for you, fading all of your elements in and out to create a seamless presentation. Animoto allows the creation of unlimited videos for free but only up to 30 seconds' duration, or a reasonably priced (£5 at the time of writing) monthly subscription for videos of up to 10 minutes in length.

If you need to create something that's more slideshow and less photographic, the Haikudeck tool, at www.haikudeck.com, is worth exploring. The menu is very simple – choose a slide type (opening slide, bullet points, text), type in your text and then choose a background – either choose block colour or get the tool to suggest a background based on the words that you have used on the slide. You can also add in graphs as well. If necessary, add in some more public notes such as links to other resources and these will be published to the web along with your deck. A brief example that I put together is at http://bit.ly/1odJme0.

Another easy to use package is MyPicPals (http://mypicpals.com), which is a slideshow generator. You can simply upload your pictures or slides, choose any special effects that you want, and you can then publish your slideshow onto Facebook, a blog, a website, etc. The interface is simplicity itself and it's extremely quick and easy to add text, choose transition styles and so on. It does work best perhaps with photographs, but there's no reason at all why you shouldn't include screenshots of, e.g. traditional PowerPoint presentation slides. If you want to see a very quick example, I uploaded some pictures of my dog Rusty at http://mypicpals.com/view-slideshow.php?sid=491081 and it probably took longer to upload the images in the first place than it did to create the presentation! If you're keen on photographic slideshows, but haven't warmed to this one, there are plenty of others to try out, such as PhotoPeach (http://photopeach.com),

Picovico at www.picovico.com/en/home (which will allow you to also add music and a theme to create a video) or Kizoa (www.kizoa.com).

Canva, at https://www.canva.com, provides a wide array of templates that are ready made for you in order to create presentations, posters, blog graphics and social media headers for your personal accounts. It's free to use if you upload your own images, but they do have over a million images available to use, though there may be a cost attached to them, which at the time of writing is US$1 each.

If you're looking for a similar concept, but one that emphasizes content and websites over photographs, then MyJugaad is a tool to try out. You can find it at http://myjugaad.in. You can either provide MyJugaad with an RSS feed of content (such as a blog), specific searches or particular websites. These can then be combined into a slideshow and used for education, bookmarking, lazy browsing or guided tours.

Animated presentations

If you're still not happy with the type of presentations that have already been mentioned, perhaps it's time to branch out a little into the world of animation. Animated presentations really bring life to what might otherwise be a rather boring or lifeless display, and they bring with them the added benefits of surprise and humour. Powtoon, at www.powtoon. com, provides both free and commercial access to its resources, enabling even a complete beginner to create an animated slide deck quickly and easily, and over 3.5 million presentations have already been created. Powtoon provides various templates such as 'explainer videos', 'school/education', 'training', and 'about us'. Alternatively, you can start from scratch to create something entirely personal. The interface does look quite complicated at the outset, as you can see in Figure 5.5, but it's actually very straightforward, with each slide in the presentation listed down the left-hand side of the screen, and a menu of animation effects down the right. Along the top of the screen are the essential items that are needed to create the presentation, such as text, sound and images. There is an almost endless supply of options, such as image holders, business animations, education, signs, social networks, shapes, backgrounds and transitions.

The ongoing animation can be saved at any point and previewed, and when it's finished it can be exported directly to YouTube for everyone to marvel at your work.

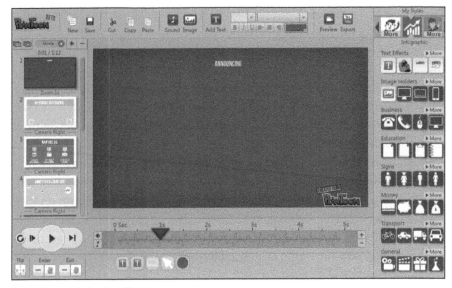

Used with permission from Powtoon

Figure 5.5 The Powtoon dashboard

Of course, not every presentation is going to work well with animated slides, so you do need to choose your subject matter accordingly, but it does make for a different approach.

Summary

In this chapter we have seen that there are many different ways of working to produce exciting, interesting and different presentations. If you still want to base your output on Microsoft PowerPoint there's no reason not to, and there are many tools that build on the work that you might have already done. Alternatively, if you want to create video presentations, animated presentations that sing and dance, or quickly create an attractive presentation with the minimum of time and effort, there are plenty of tools that help you do that as well. We have moved into a world where presentations are a real art form in themselves, and there's no reason to limit what we do to one boring bullet-pointed slide to another.

URLs mentioned in this chapter

Animoto www.animoto.com

■ Example of a presentation using Animoto
http://youtu.be/dNytmJXvd_s

AuthorStream www.authorstream.com

Brainshark https://www.brainshark.com

Canva https://www.canva.com

Capzles www.capzles.com

Dipity www.dipity.com

Emaze http://app.emaze.com

Everyslide https://everyslide.com

Haikudeck www.haikudeck.com

■ Example of a presentation using Haikudeck http://bit.ly/1odJme0

Kizoa www.kizoa.com

Knovio www.knovio.com

■ Author's presentation using Knovio http://knov.io/1dphCv6

Meograph www.meograph.com

■ Example of a presentation using Meograph http://bit.ly/1fUaAUn

MyJugaad http://myjugaad.in

MyPicPals http://mypicpals.com

■ Example of presentation using MyPicPals
http://mypicpals.com/view-slideshow.php?sid=491081

Office Mix (Microsoft) https://mix.office.com

■ Anoop Gupta, demo of interactive features in Office Mix
https://mix.office.com/watch/1v4koz7wvbove

Participoll www.participoll.com

PhotoPeach http://photopeach.com

Picovico www.picovico.com/en/home

Powtoon www.powtoon.com

Present.me https://present.me

Presentain http://presentain.com

Prezi www.prezi.com

■ Example of a Prezi presentation http://bit.ly/socmedmusic

Projeqt www.projeqt.com

Slides http://slides.com

Slideshare network www.slideshare.net

SlideTalk http://slidetalk.net

■ Slidetalk choice of voices
http://slidetalk.net/Home/VoiceSamples

Storify https://storify.com

Timeglider http://timeglider.com
Timetoast www.timetoast.com
Zentation www.zentation.com

Visit the Facet Publishing YouTube channel
(www.youtube.com/user/facetpublishing) for Phil Bradley's video
Creating great presentations without using PowerPoint.

CHAPTER 6

Teaching and training

Introduction

Most of us, at some time in our working careers, are involved in teaching things to other people. It may be a part of our job as a school or college/university librarian, we may need to run induction sessions for colleagues, or it might be necessary to teach a member of the public how to set their privacy settings on Facebook. Often this training is done face to face, and that's generally the best way of working; you're available to ask and answer specific questions from the trainee, you can easily check to see if they understand what is being said, and you can do a demonstration for them. However, there may be times when you aren't available, or someone needs to learn something at a time when it isn't possible for a member of staff to run a session, or you may have to run exactly the same session several times, which can be tedious and lead to a less-than-expert presentation.

It's at times like this that social media tools can make your job a lot easier, and in this chapter I'll be looking at some of the ways that you can teach people when you cannot run a face-to-face presentation and I'll look at some of the other things that you can do to assist the learning process.

Screencasting

The concept behind screencasting is very simple. You record what is happening on your computer screen, narrate it in some way – perhaps by text, audio recording or webcam video – and make it available for people to view at a time that works for them. Some of the tools will simply capture what you are doing in a browser window, others will capture anything that you are doing on the desktop. Some you have to register for, others you can simply use by clicking a button and others again have to be downloaded and installed. As with all of the other tools mentioned in this book, they are free, although some will have a commercial element if you wish to use some of their advanced features.

Quick and easy tools

Screencast-o-matic, www.screencast-o-matic.com, is about as simple as it is possible to get when it comes to screencasting. The home page has a very large 'Start Recording' button on it. You can simply click on this to begin the recording, although it does require a Java plug-in to run. If you cannot install that, or are not allowed to, you can download and install their app instead. Before the recording starts you are presented with a frame that you can move and resize to record anything on your screen – so this could be a web search, a guided tour of different websites or a tutorial on how to use Microsoft Word, for example. You can also choose a microphone to use if you wish to create an audio narrative, and you can also record from a webcam. You can pause or restart if necessary, and you just click 'Done' when you have finished, and can then save the recording directly to the Screencast-o-matic site, or publish on YouTube, or save as a video file. The free version has a number of limitations, not least of which is that you cannot edit your work (so don't do anything on a day when you are suffering from a cold or bad cough), and you are limited to the length of screencast that you can record. The Pro version allows users to edit the video with cut, zoom, blur, text overlays and so on, and has an unlimited maximum recording time. At the time of writing the Pro version costs US$15 a year.

Screenr, at www.screenr.com, works in a very similar way; it has a record button that you can just click on, but again you need to have the Java plug-in installed and it won't work without it; if it's not available Screenr will prompt you and offer a link to a download location. Assuming that everything is correct, however, you can create a recording up to five minutes in length. As with Screencast-o-matic, you can choose the size of the recording window and a microphone source if you want an audio narration. Screenr will host the recording and you can host it on YouTube, download it as an .mp4 file and link to it from Facebook and Twitter.

Various commercial options are available, from 'Lite' through to 'Enterprise'.

There are, of course, various other tools that work in exactly the same way, such as Apowersoft recorder (www.apowersoft.com/free-online-screen-recorder), Screen Recorder (www.screenvideorecorder.net) or ScreenCastle (http://screencastle.com).

Download packages

While some of the online packages are quite sophisticated, they are often limited in the amount that you can do with them, especially in the area of editing. Another drawback which I have already mentioned is that they tend to work with the Java application, which is a separate piece of software. Unfortunately, as there are security scares around this on a regular basis, your technical support department may not be too keen on you using it. Consequently you might find that a package that you download to use will actually be more useful in the long run. There are a few packages that I think are particularly worth exploring; they tend to be more powerful, with lots of functionality and don't require an internet connection to create a video.

BB FlashBack Express can be found at www.bbsoftware.co.uk as a free download. When the tool is used you start by choosing the size of the screen to record, and as usual this may be a section of a web browser screen, or it could be another software package completely – very useful if you want to teach people how to use a database or catalogue, for example. You can choose to record an audio narration to go with it, and you can also use a webcam, so that viewers can see you as well. Once you have recorded your presentation (which can be as long as you wish) you can save it, and then review it with the editing tool. This allows you to see your recorded activities frame by frame, making it really easy to edit out anything that you don't want. A trick that I have found useful is that if you make an error or cough, carry on recording for a few moments without doing or saying anything. That makes the error much easier to spot when you are reviewing the recording, and you can then easily edit out the error and splice in the rest of the recording quite naturally. Once you have edited your screencast and are happy with it, you can then save it and upload it to a video-sharing site. BB Flashback is my preferred solution, and you can see an example of the way in which it works on a short video that I produced on the dangers of clicking on e-mail links at http://youtu.be/JYyt9Q9MFzU. The free version probably does everything that most people will want to do, but the standard and professional versions do have extra functionality to provide more annotation, add images and improve on the editing function. If you're unhappy with the functionality provided by BB Flashback, however, you might want to explore Jing, which is produced by TechSmith and can be located at www.techsmith.com/jing.html.

Screencapture

There will be plenty of times when all you want to do is to capture a screenshot, to incorporate into a training manual or to put in a poster, for example. Some of the tools mentioned previously (such as Jing) do provide this functionality as part of their offer, but there are other tools that specialize in this. There are a number of things that you'll need to consider when choosing a tool – do you just need to capture the screen that you can see, or do you need to be able to capture an entire web page? Does the tool enable you to capture a smaller part of the screen, and can it be used to blur the background? Can you annotate the screenshot to add in text or shapes, or to use a freehand pen?

At the very simplest level if you are using a Windows-based computer you probably already have a tool available to you – the Snipping tool, which looks like a pair of scissors, as you can see from Figure 6.1, which is the icon.

Figure 6.1 Windows toolbar with Snipping tool icon

You can use the basic tools that come with the program to highlight and add freehand marking, as demonstrated in Figure 6.2. However, it's not a particularly elegant tool, but works well in a pinch; indeed, if all you need is a quick screenshot, that might be the best answer for you. As you would expect, though, there are far better tools that you can use, but they're all programs that you download or install onto your browser as add-ons – it depends entirely on your requirements. If you just need to take shots of

Figure 6.2 Elements of the Snipping tool

web pages, a browser add-on will do all that's necessary.

TinyTake (http://tinytake.com) is a free capture tool that works in a Windows environment, and has to be downloaded. It has a wide number of options allowing users to annotate their screenshots with boxes, with text in different colours and freehand. The screencapture can then be saved online and shared across social media or sent by e-mail. SnapCrab for Windows, at www.fenrir-inc.com/us/snapcrab, is very similar to TinyTake, but it makes a very satisfying camera-style shutter closing sound as you take the image. You can save files in different formats, exclude the mouse cursor, and share across social media. The tool that I use myself (which may or may not appeal to you) is called Awesome Screenshot Plus and it's a browser add-on for Firefox at https://addons.mozilla.org/en-US/firefox/addon/awesome-screenshot-capture-/developers. It sits on the browser as a bookmarklet icon and is available to be clicked when required. The screenshot is displayed with a small menu of options to crop, create shapes, arrows, lines, freehand, blur parts of the screen and add text. The image can then be saved online at the Awesome Screenshot site, where it will remain for about a month, or alternatively it can be downloaded as a file or saved permanently onto Diigo.com, which is a bookmarking service. This last option is the reason that I find it particularly useful, because I also use Diigo to save and share material; the blending of both tools together is very effective and saves me a lot of time.

A slightly different approach is Szoter (http://szoter.com), which is designed for users to upload pictures or take screenshots, annotate them, add text and save them in order to share with other people. You can scale, rotate, sketch, adjust colours, crop the workspace and so on – it's essentially a graphics package focused on screenshots.

Interactive training: Google+ Hangouts

Running a training course where you cannot interact with the people that you are training is not an ideal situation, of course, and it's usually far better if you can actually work with them in a live situation. Google Hangouts is obviously an excellent choice here, and we've discussed this in Chapter 5, but as a brief reminder you can talk face to face, you can share your computer screen with the people who are in the Hangout with you, and you can also run a slideshow presentation by using the Google Hangouts Slideshare application. Google Hangouts offers the option of hosting a Hangout Party, which is a situation in which you can interact with up to nine other people, and only those people can watch or listen to the conversation. The other option is a Hangout on Air, where you can record the entire discussion that you've been having and place it onto YouTube (and you can also share the discussion live as well). While this does have obvious advantages, I don't think that this helps when training, since you want your delegates to feel safe and secure and confident enough to ask those 'really silly' questions which are often the most important. If they know that other people might be, in a sense, eavesdropping, or that their lack of knowledge will be on display for the world to see, that makes it much less likely that they will want to contribute at the same level.

Before starting a course there are a few things that you'll need to check. First of all, you have to make sure that all of the participants can actually get into the Hangout in the first place. They will need a Google+ account and will need a browser and operating system that supports video calls. (Current details are available on the Google+ help page 'Hangouts system requirements' at https://support.google.com/plus/answer/1216376?hl=en) The first time that a computer is used for a Hangout, Google does need to install a small piece of software, so the system will need to be capable of this, or it might be necessary to get a technical support person to authorize it. While it's not essential to have a webcam and/or microphone it's helpful, so that you can see everyone, and everyone can see each other. The amount of bandwidth required varies, but it can be adjusted according to each participant's network, with a minimum bandwidth of 256kbps and an ideal bandwidth of 3mbps for a session with up to 10 people. More details are available on the Google+ help page 'Bandwidth setting' at https://support.google.com/plus/answer/2979333. Ideally for your own peace of mind it's an idea to check with each delegate well in advance of the training session to make sure that their connection works, and that they're familiar with using a Hangout. It does take a little more of your time as a trainer, but in the long run you'll save more time if you don't have to ask other participants to wait while you try and sort out a technical issue. I would also suggest that if you're the trainer you should put all of your trainees into a specific Google+ circle to make it easier to connect with them on the day of the course. One final thing that is worth checking out is the environment in which you'll be doing the training. Make sure that you have a nice quiet room with a 'do not disturb' sign on the door, since the last thing you want is for a colleague to make an unexpected arrival. Take a look at the background behind you, and make sure that it's as neat as possible, with no distractions; there's nothing as offputting to both trainer and delegate as to see someone peering past your shoulder at something in the room or out of the window! You might wish to invest in a cheap screen of some sort so that the rest of the room is blocked off. Also turn off or mute your phones – we're used to doing this with mobile phones during courses, but it's all too easy to forget that you probably have a phone next to you on the desk, and you'll only remember when it starts ringing loudly.

There is little point in going into any great detail about the actual process required to start a Hangout, since it's entirely possible this will change between my writing and your reading. However, the process will be fairly straightforward, giving you the opportunity to start a Hangout Party, give it a name and invite people to join. Once the Hangout has started you will want to schedule appropriate breaks, unless the session is quite short. It might be helpful to have an assistant, if you have enough room, who can take care of any technical issues, make a note of questions, action points and so on; while you may be able to do this normally in a face-to-face training event, it's rather more difficult in a Hangout! Hopefully your delegates will already have a copy of your handout, but if not, then you can share this with them via a file on your Google Drive account. You can also include other documents and files during the course of the training session, as necessary. It's worth constantly remembering that Google owns YouTube, so it makes sense to use videos that you already have in your YouTube channel. There is an app in the Hangouts options that everyone should have, as it allows them all to see the video being played. Anyone can pause a video, and everyone will see that the video has been paused, but voices are muted while a video is playing. It's worth revisiting the available apps to see if Google has added anything new; while the future of the Google+ network is the subject of some doubt, I think it's fair to say that Hangouts is such a useful function that it's unlikely that it's going to disappear any time soon.

If you want to go down the route of a Google+ Hangout on Air, the process is not too dissimilar to that which has just been discussed. There may well be times when you want to save a training video or webinar, particularly if you have a lot of frequently asked questions about some aspect of the library, or queries focused around searching databases, induction and so on. Since this Hangout is going to be recorded you may want to structure it rather more tightly, and pre-plan questions and answers with your participants, or you may wish to have it entirely structured by including other members of staff. Don't forget that once the Hangout has finished that's just the first part of the story – you will want to promote the session using various other social media outlets and embed it in your blog and on your website, as well as in any online training resources that you have.

Interactive training: other resources

You may prefer not to use Google+ as a training platform, and by now I expect that you already realize that if there's an application that supports a particular activity there's going to be rather more than one. An alternative that you may wish to explore is WizIQ, which you can find at www.wiziq.com. It's a global platform which offers a course delivery solution for teachers and trainers, as well as traditional academic users. It currently has over 250,000 active educators and 3.5 million registered users in over 100 countries. Users work in a virtual classroom which simulates the face-to-face experience by offering real-time audiovisual communication, polls, video and text chatting, breakout rooms, interactive whiteboards and screensharing. Teachers can give tests and quizzes, students can be surveyed and group work and tasks can be conducted. WizIQ offers a free version which has some limitations, as well as two professional plans.

Alternatively Edmodo (https://www.edmodo.com) may appeal – it was founded in 2008 and has over 35 million members around the world. Accounts can be created by teachers, parents or students. You can create learning groups and invite people to join, then share work with that group, adding interactive quizzes and polls, for example. The emphasis is on school-age groups, but there is an option for higher education which in most cases would be the appropriate one to use when working with adults. Blackboard (previously known as Elluminate), at www.blackboard.com, offers a collaborative, interactive and mobile learning environment, with virtual classrooms, offices and meeting spaces.

Pixiclip, at www.pixiclip.com/beta, is an online, interactive whiteboard that you can use to communicate using a webcam or microphone. Users can record their screen and share it with others, and you can type, narrate, scribble and include images that you can then mark up and work with. The whole process can be recorded, saved and shared by linking or embedding. It can be used to create a how-to guide, to share instructional videos with people who can then watch them whenever they need to, or for students to make their own book trailers, for example. It's a very simple tool to use and it's web- and browser-based, so nothing has to be downloaded.

MOOCs

A MOOC is one of the more recent additions to the internet pantheon of obscure abbreviations – it stands for 'Massive Open Online Course'. While it's probably unlikely that librarians would want to start their own MOOC, it's worth briefly spending a few minutes discussing them, since you may wish to join one, or to advise a library member on them. They emerged in 2012 and are intended to provide unlimited participation and open access; training materials such as videos, readings and interactive forums allow students and teachers to discuss the content of the course and to share thoughts and experiences. Courses can be organized by high-profile universities, some for a fee leading to credits, while others are created by people who are passionate about a particular subject and are for general education and enjoyment. The UK's Open University launched a British MOOC provider Futurelearn (https://www.futurelearn.com), which currently has 36 UK and international university partners, as well as the British Museum, British Library and British Council. Courses cover such areas as 'How to give a great presentation', 'Medicines adherence:

supporting patients with their treatment' and 'Web science: how the web is changing the world'. Another example is Coursera, at https://www. coursera.org, which has partnered with many top universities to offer over 600 free courses.

Many MOOCs use video lectures with the addition of peer review and group collaboration and automated feedback through objective assessments such as online quizzes and examinations. Completion rates are generally quite low, often 10% or less, as many registered students explore the topic rather than completing an entire course. Depending on the ethos behind the MOOC, this may or may not be viewed as a success or failure.

Advantages and disadvantages of e-learning

The basic concepts of teaching and learning don't depend on the environment being used: you basically take the knowledge that you have, and share it with other people who want to (or perhaps have to!) obtain it themselves. There is no single 'best' way of doing this; there are, as we have seen, plenty of different approaches. However, when we introduce methods of teaching and learning using the tools that have already been mentioned, we do need to consider what effect these have on both processes.

E-learning is a very convenient way for people to learn – they don't have to physically be in the same place as the trainer, who could be on the other side of the world in some cases, and therefore this has a helpful side-effect in reducing travelling costs. If the training session is recorded learners can view it whenever they want to, stopping and starting whenever is appropriate; they can log on and complete work or view videos whenever they wish to. It also means that unless the course is live it's available to be run at any time, which means that the trainer can produce the materials once and then simply allow a course to run when it's appropriate, simply by giving delegates access to the materials when needed.

However, these advantages are balanced by the disadvantages. People do prefer to be physically in front of a trainer; not only is the interaction greater, but there are all of the intangibles, such as informal chats at tea breaks and the relaxed networking opportunities. Students may also feel disengaged, from each other and from the trainer, since the opportunities for questions and answers may be limited – certainly so in recorded sessions. It's therefore difficult for the trainer to fully appreciate if their materials make sense to students or whether they merely confuse or frustrate them. Students may also have problems if they don't have access to all the benefits of modern technology, such as fast broadband, webcams and microphones.

This type of training will therefore not be appropriate for everyone, but it's certainly worth considering if it's the best way for you as a trainer to teach a group of people, either as a one-off, or as part of your general day-to-day work.

Summary

As an increasing number of tools and resources become available to all of us, the world can paradoxically become more complicated, rather than less. While tools make our lives easier there is a limit on how simple they can be, and the more powerful the tool, the more time it takes to learn it effectively. If we accept (as I think we should) that information professionals are in the business of empowering their communities, this means that we need to teach them how to use the resources at their disposal. Consequently I firmly believe that our role will increasingly involve teaching and training. In order to do this effectively we have to first train ourselves by exploring the tools that are available, so that we can in turn teach others.

URLs mentioned in this chapter

Apowersoft recorder www.apowersoft.com/free-online-screen-recorder

Awesome Screenshot Plus https://addons.mozilla.org/en-US/firefox/
addon/awesome-screenshot-capture-/developers

BB FlashBack Express www.bbsoftware.co.uk

■ Example of BB Flashback http://youtu.be/JYyt9Q9MFzU

Blackboard www.blackboard.com

Coursera https://www.coursera.org

Edmodo https://www.edmodo.com

Futurelearn https://www.futurelearn.com

Google Hangouts system requirements
https://support.google.com/plus/answer/1216376?hl=en

Google+ help page 'Bandwidth setting'
https://support.google.com/plus/answer/2979333

Pixiclip www.pixiclip.com/beta

Screen Recorder www.screenvideorecorder.net

ScreenCastle http://screencastle.com

Screencast-o-matic www.screencast-o-matic.com

Screenr www.screenr.com

SnapCrab for Windows www.fenrir-inc.com/us/snapcrab

Szoter http://szoter.com

TechSmith www.techsmith.com/jing.html

TinyTake http://tinytake.com

WizIQ www.wiziq.com

Visit the Facet Publishing YouTube channel
www.youtube.com/user/facetpublishing) for Phil Bradley's video
A guide to hosting Google hangouts.

CHAPTER 7

Communication

Introduction

In 'the old days' people had physically to come into the library to get the information that they needed. Since we were working in a situation when the content and the artefact were inextricably linked, this is not surprising. However, with the advent of CD-ROM networking technology it became much easier for librarians to put information directly onto the desks of the people who needed to use it. Our role then needed to include much more training, because we couldn't see what people were doing – in the library, if they made an error, it was much easier for them just to ask us, or we could see they were having difficulties. However, if the CEO at her desk was trying to find something and couldn't, she might be less inclined to view the benefits of these technologies favourably. Consequently, the process of moving information out of the library and onto desktops was linked to various activities – not just making it easier to find information, but to teach people how to use the materials (hardware and software) and also to promote and strengthen the value of the library service.

Little changed in the interim, except perhaps 'more' – more information, more people and more to promote to a wider audience. We can't expect people to come into the library any longer – we have to go out to them, and remember that 'Outside the library is still the library', as Stephen Abram has put it (www.slideshare.net/stephenabram1/fort-bend-tx-may-2013-staff-day). In other words, we need to go to where the conversations are; we cannot expect them to come to us. Therefore we need to look at the different types of communication that we want to have with our members and then decide where they can best take place, identify the tools and then get involved. In this chapter we'll look at what we want to say, who we want to say it to, how we want to say it and when we want to say it.

'Just the facts'

There are plenty of times when all that you need to do is to communicate one way to tell your members something, and there's little discussion to be had about it. For example, your physical address, your website address, contact details, opening hours and so on. Your website has always been the best place to put this type of information; the communication is all one way, with the organization putting the facts out there for people to take. Ideally the site will provide added value whenever possible – rather than just the address of the organization it will include a map of how to get there, for example.

The website should be the basis of all of the communication that the organization does, which is not to say that all of the communication should go through the website – quite the opposite in fact. However, it's sensible to provide website visitors with links and access to all of the social media accounts the library has available. If searchers find one social media account it should drive them directly to all of the others, so the website should really be right at the centre of the web, as it were. It makes sense to incorporate other social media activities onto the website when possible, and so, for example, rather than just link to the Twitter account, perhaps include a live feed so that all of the tweets that are sent out also appear on the appropriate page on the website. This also has the added value that website content can be changed via a third party application; if the snow is too thick to get to work, it's then easy enough to use the Twitter account to say that the library will be closed for the day; timely and accurate information quickly delivered.

In the past the website really was one of the very few ways of getting information out to library members and other interested people, so there was understandably a lot of reliance on it. There is a whole industry built on the importance of the website: website designers, search engine optimizers – even Google is built on the concept that the website is essentially the be-all and end-all of the web. Now, of course, we know that is no longer the case, and user-generated content far outstrips what goes onto websites. Unfortunately, however, a lot of the people in middle and senior management may well not appreciate this and still subscribe to the idea that everything needs to be done on the website. That is not where the people that you want to communicate with are going to be, though – they may do a quick 'drive-by' to get the basics, but will then be moving on again if they want to interact with someone from the organization. It's therefore really important to go to where the conversations are; if you don't explore conversation tools such as Twitter those conversations will still be taking place there – it's just that you won't have an opportunity to engage with them.

In summary – don't ignore or forget the website, but instead incorporate it into everything that you are doing when using social media, but make it a basis from which you extend outwards (both in terms of communication and the way you communicate), rather than the only way that you try to communicate.

Twitter

Twitter is of course one of the basic tools that people think of when it comes to communicating. I can't imagine that there is a single reader who hasn't heard of Twitter, since it's both the darling and the bête noire of mainstream media. However, there are a considerable number of people who really haven't delved into it yet, or who are not convinced of its value.

I first heard about Twitter at a conference about seven years ago, and one businessman was explaining to another what it was used for. He said that it was useful because he could tell people where he was at any moment in the day. I really couldn't see the point of that at all! However, I got an account and set it up and very soon realized that it was actually a rather helpful microblogging site, enabling me to send text messages (tweets) up to 140 characters in length. Twitter was created in March 2006 and by 2012 had over 500 million registered users. Tweets are now posted at the rate of over 200,000 per minute, with 1.6 billion search queries per day (see http://en.wikipedia.org/wiki/Twitter). People tweet about all manner of things – what they are doing, where they are going, when they have blogged, information on breaking news stories, quotes from conference speakers, thoughts, ideas and opinions. Twitter is unfairly criticized for being 'full of rubbish', but the same could be said of any other communication medium; however, with Twitter you can quickly sort through what you consider to be rubbish and remove it. Twitter users follow other people (in much the same way that they do on Facebook) and will see their tweets in their tweet stream or timeline. If people are posting rubbish, it's easy to unfollow them, reducing the nonsense that you are seeing. Rather than focus on criticisms of the resource, however, let's concentrate on how it can best be used within a library setting.

There are primarily four different ways that Twitter can be used, and they are not mutually exclusive.

Twitter as a broadcasting tool

Tweets can be used to simply broadcast a piece of information which may be something as prosaic as early closing on Friday, or it might be a celebrity providing information about an upcoming tour. The effectiveness of this approach really does depend on the number of people who are following that particular account. In the case of the celebrity it may well be many millions, and this can be a very effective approach of communicating from one to many. However, if you are tweeting as a library, it's unlikely that you'll have that many followers, and if that type of one-way communication is all you are doing with Twitter, you probably won't get many more. It can, nevertheless, be a very useful way of updating a static web page with information which will be seen by people who go to the library website home page. In that situation I'd suggest having a Twitter account that is used primarily for that purpose, and while it's useful to publicize it, there's little point in worrying about how many followers it has.

Twitter for lurking

Twitter can also be used in 'lurk mode', which is to say that you create an account specifically designed to follow lots of people just to see what they are saying and to keep up to date with the news in your area of interest. The key issue here is to make sure that you follow the right people, and there are a variety of ways in which you can do this. Firstly I would suggest running some searches for references to your library or organization to see who is tweeting about it, use sites such as We Follow (www.wefollow.com) to identify experts and people of influence on Twitter, try some searches at SocialMention* (www.socialmention.com) to find more people and other terms that you can search on, and slowly build up a following list of people who are posting good-quality content on a regular basis. If you just wish to lurk it doesn't really matter how many people follow you back (so we have the exact opposite of the previous scenario, when the number of followers was paramount), although of course a few will.

Twitter and two-way communication

The third approach to using Twitter, and the one that will probably be most attractive, is to use it as a means of two-way communication – you want to listen to what people say, but also interact with them as well. In order for this to work well you have to build up a collection of people that you are following, but equally, make sure that you are being followed back by other people – hopefully in similar numbers. This is not something that will happen overnight, and it does take hard work and perseverance, but over the course of time Twitter will become one of the most powerful communication tools that you have at your disposal. Before starting on this particular journey it's really necessary to decide why you're tweeting, who you are tweeting to, and who in the library is going to be doing it! The worst thing that you can possibly do is to set up an account and not really have any idea of what you're going to do with it; that will become self-evident very quickly and will not encourage people to follow the account. There is nothing to stop you having one account and sharing the user name and password with colleagues, but that does mean that it's necessary to have a consistent approach to what and how you're tweeting; type of information, the use of shorthand, level of humour (or lack of it) and so on.

There are various metrics circulating around the internet on tweeting ratios. For example, there is 5-3-2, which breaks down into: 5 tweets are content from other people, 3 tweets are content from you, and 2 tweets are personal/organizational in nature. Alternatively there is the 4-1-1 approach; 4 pieces of relevant and original content from other people and 1 retweet of someone else's material for every self-serving update. Then there is the 'golden ratio' of 3-6-1, which is 3 pieces of your information, 6 pieces of curated content, and 1 piece of promotional material. While the numbers are all different the concept is the same; provide good-quality information for the people who are following you, and dial back on promotional material. This may not seem to make sense, especially if you're just starting out on Twitter, because surely people follow you because they want to hear what you have to say? While that's true, by providing good-quality information and links to other resources you're also actually talking about yourself or your library, only you're saying 'I think this is really helpful information', and you gain a reputation for curating helpful material. If you can help or inform other people, they will want to follow you, and to engage with you.

It's worth looking at what other libraries are doing on Twitter, just to get something of a feel for how they are using it. You can go onto Twitter and search for library accounts of course, but I have a small (300+) list of library Twitter accounts that you might want to look at, which you can find at https://twitter.com/Philbradley/lists/libraries. Some examples of tweets relate to books of the week, new DVDs, links to professional articles, photographs of library events, conversations back and forth with other people or libraries, jokes, news items and so on. In other words – a total mish-mash of content, but all of it designed to inform, engage or entertain. The language used is also quite informal; it's worth remembering that Twitter is an informal medium; since space is limited people often tweet in shorthand to cram more into their 140 characters. Formal communication does of course have its place, but that's probably on the website, and unless your tweets are from a particularly formal organization some levity is usually appreciated.

It is important to engage with people on Twitter – if they refer to you in a tweet, then it's worthwhile acknowledging it, and enter a conversation with them. You shouldn't be afraid about starting conversations either – if you want to know how another library does something for example, then simply ask, and hopefully you'll get a quick response. If there's something that is in the news, and you have something helpful that could be added, tweet about it. There is I think an unnecessary concern that somehow having a Twitter account will open up the library to criticism, and I've seen this used as an excuse for not having an account. It's certainly true that at times people will tweet critical comments, but isn't it better to be able to see them, and to be in a position to respond, rather than let the criticism go unchecked? As I've already said – go to where the conversations are, and that also includes less than complimentary material.

I briefly mentioned the idea of Twitter lists, and this is a very useful tool which is remarkably under-used. You can create lists for any group of people that you're following (and indeed people that you're not), although you cannot tweet out a message to that specific list; it's just for reading tweets, not for responding to them. You could choose to create lists of members or users of your library or information service, other similar library accounts, other librarians, subject specialists or competitors, for example.

It's also important to know when to tweet material out. Clearly not all of the people who follow your account will be on Twitter at the same moment in time, so you need to decide on the best time of day to publish material in order to get the largest exposure possible. Tweriod, at www.tweriod.com, can help with this. Connect your Twitter account to Tweriod and it will give you a series of handy graphs based on the last 1000 of your followers; it is generated according to the timezone you have on your Twitter.com profile. It will give you various charts for weekends, Mondays, weekdays and combined times. My own set of charts indicated that the best time of day for me to tweet was at about 2 p.m. on weekdays; perhaps people ease themselves back into work after lunch by catching up on Twitter? It is also worth considering if and when tweets should be repeated; what about those people who like to ease themselves into work by checking Twitter when they first sit down at their desks, or who check it last thing before leaving work? If you have a particularly important tweet, it may be worth tweeting it first at 2 p.m. on a Monday, then 9 a.m. on a Tuesday and at 4 p.m. on a Wednesday, for example. That way you will get a good cross-section of followers, and hopefully not many of them will see the tweet repeated several times.

The science of tweeting does not stop at that point, however. Shorter tweets are much more likely to receive engagement than those of over 100 characters, and if the tweet is short it makes it easier for people to retweet (where someone takes your tweet and reposts it out to all of their followers, pushing your message out further), rather than having to edit it down to send on. Unsurprisingly, if you include a request that the tweet should be retweeted, it's more likely that will happen, but such requests should be fairly rare, or people will get irritated and less likely to comply. The use of hashtags is also a good way to engage with people. Hashtags are a very simple concept, but they do cause a lot of confusion as well. A hashtag is essentially a controlled vocabulary term, but as defined by individual users. If people are tweeting about the Chartered Institute of Library and Information Professionals they may well use the hashtag #cilip somewhere in the tweet, or if they are particularly irate about something on the BBC 'Question Time' programme they may use #bbcqt. If searchers then want to find out who has been tweeting about something they can simply search on an appropriate hashtag to see all of the tweets that mention it, irrespective of the people doing the tweeting. It's a very powerful tool if you want to keep up with what people are tweeting about – at a conference, for example

– hopefully the conference organizer will be suggesting that people use a particular hashtag to tweet reports and quotes, making it easier for everyone to follow along. There are no official rules about hashtags – some people will use them to emphasis a particular point, such as #saturdaylibrarian for example, or #joking as a way of underlining what they're doing. Anyone can use a hashtag, and you can put the hashtag anywhere in the tweet that you wish – beginning, middle or end. It helps if you don't use more than two hashtags in any one tweet, or you won't have any room for the actual message! You may decide that you want to use a hashtag when tweeting about what the library is doing, for any promotional tweets, or if you are asking people to retweet what you have sent out in order to track to see how far the tweet actually goes.

Twitter for search

The final way in which people can use Twitter is as a search tool. Given that we are approaching 300,000 tweets per minute, this is a huge firehose of information, and it's increasingly being used to break news stories: a wide variety of organizations, such as police forces and media outlets, use Twitter. If I have to find an expert in a particular area I'll almost certainly search Twitter to see who is talking about that particular subject, and I'll check out their biography to see where they come from, what they tweet about, and how many people follow them. If you or your library have a particular expertise or reputation in a subject area it makes sense to tweet about it in exactly the same way that you might send out a press release or create a web page. If you are not doing that, it doesn't mean that the conversations won't take place, they will simply take place without your involvement. Twitter's own search engine is not terribly useful, and a better option would be to use Topsy (www.topsy.com), which provides searchers with access to a database of over 425 billion tweets, going back to Twitter's earliest days.

In fact, not only is the Twitter search option fairly poor, the entire interface is hardly up to scratch, and I suspect that this puts a lot of people off before they have even had an opportunity to try it out properly. However, other tools are available which make the whole process of using Twitter much more bearable, and far easier. Hootsuite, at https://hootsuite.com, is one such example. Rather than having a simple timeline, with all of the tweets appearing chronologically, Hootsuite encourages the use of columns. So you may have one column for all of the tweets that the people you follow send out, another column for references to your Twitter handle, another for a particular hashtag, one for specific individuals, and yet another for the results of a particular search string. By breaking the tweets down like this they become much more manageable and far easier to follow. If you don't find Hootsuite to your taste you may prefer to try out Tweetdeck, at https://tweetdeck.twitter.com, which used to be an independent tool, but has now been purchased by Twitter itself.

Facebook

Facebook (https://en.gb.facebook.com) is of course the 800lb gorilla of social media. It's almost pointless to provide facts and figures because they're going to be out of date before I finish typing the sentence, let alone when the book is published. However, there are a minimum of 1.23 billion monthly active users, 66% of millennials (people between 15 and 34) use it, and 20 minutes per day is the average amount of time spent on the site. If that's not enough for you, 243,000 photographs are uploaded every minute, over 3 million items are shared, over 300 days of YouTube videos are watched and over 50,000 links are shared.

Let's be clear at the outset – Facebook is not about friends any longer. It may have been once, a very long time ago, but it's now used as a tool by a very wide variety of businesses to market, promote and interact with clients, fans, friends and members. One only has to take a look at advertisements in the press, on the radio or on television – there are a decreasing number of links to a website and an increase in the amount of links to a Facebook page. There are many consumer brands that measure their fan numbers on Facebook in the tens of millions. In 2011 Coca Cola had 22 million Facebook fans but in June of 2014 that number had risen to over 84 million. Significantly, the visitors to their website are continuing to fall; by more than 40% in a 12-month period (www.jeffbullas.com/2011/03/21/is-facebook-killing-off-the-company-website).

It might be tempting to ask the question 'Should my library or company just have a Facebook page, then?' but that's really the wrong question – we need to be looking at activity rather than tool: Facebook is a tool to support the activity, and not the other way around. A better question would be to ask 'What can my Facebook page do for my library or company that my website or other social media tools cannot do?' I think that the clear answer here is that it Facebook can be used to communicate in an entirely different way to that of the website. Your website is the traditional brick wall with information spray-painted onto it. There is no engagement, no interaction and no way of communicating back and forth. In most instances visitors can look at what's there, take note of it, and then leave. While that is communication of sorts, it's not engaging or interesting.

In order to use Facebook effectively as a communications tool there are a number of things that you really have to consider. First of all, it's obviously necessary to have a page for your group, library or organization. The banner needs to be clear, the avatar or small 'icon' has to be recognized – ideally it should be exactly the same one that you are using on other social media platforms, to ensure a level of consistency. A good 'About' section, basic information, location and contact details all need to be filled in. It's going to be necessary to decide if you wish to have a page that has an umbrella approach, such as Essex Libraries (https://www.facebook.com/EssexLibraries), which has a Facebook page that covers all of its libraries but individual libraries within the county have their own pages as well.

Who is going to be responsible for the page? It's very tempting for a press, publicity or communications department to want to have control, but I feel that is a fatal error, because they are not the people on the front line, dealing with library members on a day-to-day basis. They are not going to be the people who know what followers or fans are interested in, or how to keep their attention. They may well counter by saying that employees should not take over their role, but if we once again refer back to 'activity, not tool', it's the role of the information professionals to communicate with their members, not the press or communications department. Figure 7.1 shows a snippet of the Essex Libraries Facebook page.

The Facebook page needs to be inviting, enjoyable and interesting. Equally importantly, it's necessary to make sure that the content that is shared is going to be reshared by your fans to their friends, family and contacts. Original content is really important at this point, particularly if it includes photographs. Post frequently about newsworthy material; because of the way that Facebook works, you cannot be certain that all of your posts will be seen by all of your fans – in fact it's certainly not going to be the case, as Facebook 'throttles' posts and doesn't automatically share them with everyone. [It may come as something of a surprise, but simply posting to your group page will not mean that everyone who subscribes to it will see that particular post. Facebook has taken it upon itself to decide what to show to which subscribers. You can test this out for yourself – choose one of the Facebook

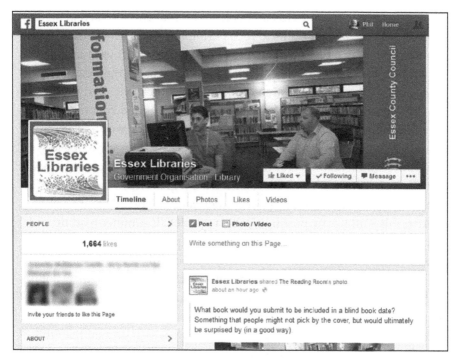

Figure 7.1 Essex Libraries Facebook page

groups that you have joined and look through your own timeline to see its posts, then go directly to the group page. In all likelihood you'll see other posts there which Facebook didn't automatically share with you.]

Share content that allows fans to inform other people about the things they care about; if you are a public librarian it makes sense to write about local events, history, facts and figures. If you are a corporate librarian, post about subject-specific material in order to inform and entertain. Facebook users like to share content in order to indicate to the people that they connect with about their interests, cares and concerns; it also allows them to support causes that they feel strongly about.

A Facebook page needs to be active – there is nothing more off-putting than looking for a particular page only to find that it's moribund; that sends out such a negative message it's better not to have a page in the first instance. Comment on other people's pages where your target audience is already having conversations, and link to related pages – other libraries, local businesses or academic organizations, for example. The writing style should be natural; formality is best left on the website. People don't expect a formal style when it comes to Facebook; jokes, chat and interaction are the order of the day; no one wants to read boring posts. This also means that emotions can play a part on the page; be passionate about your interests because your fans are – that's why they liked the page in the first place. Write posts that engage, question, challenge readers – you want to establish a good rapport with your fans and get their thoughts and comments. Consequently ask them for their opinions; rather than a post that says 'these are the ten best fiction books according to Amazon' (or whoever), ask for their recommendations for their favourite titles in a particular genre and compile your own top ten. Calls to action are a great way of engaging people. Cheshire Public Library asked their fans to 'spread the love of reading this summer by posting a selfie with YOUR summer reading and using the hashtag #cplsummerreadingself' (https://www.facebook.com/cheshirelibrary/posts/10152514300455513:0). Not only is this involving people, it's asking for visual engagement (which is always popular) and it's using a hashtag which people can then search on.

Unlike Twitter, it's best to use full URLs when posting links to external websites, since shortened links get three times less engagement than full ones. People like to know exactly where they are going – while they may put up with it on Twitter, Facebook isn't Twitter and shouldn't be treated as such.

Finally, it's very important to be yourself. There's no reason why a post shouldn't start with 'So and So here today', because it's a clear indication that different members of the library are involved with Facebook, and by implication with the page fans.

A comment that is often made to me about interacting with people is that there is the danger of negative comments. That's perfectly true, but if people are going to write negative things, there are plenty of places that they can do it and they probably will. However, if someone posts a negative comment onto a Facebook page, that's almost always a clear indication that they want to engage with someone in order to get a reaction or a situation resolved. Opening up a Facebook page to comments doesn't increase hostility, it actually goes a long way to mitigating it. If the criticism is valid, then it can be addressed, an apology made and an indication of what will happen differently in the future can be shown. This is a mature approach that illustrates professionalism and respect for the person making the initial comment. Of course, if the complaint is inaccurate that point can be made, and the person politely corrected. That also shows a mature and professional approach, so we have a win-win situation. Sometimes people will continue an aggressive attitude; they become 'trolls' and these do need a rather different approach, because they are less interested in having a problem sorted out and more interested in just being a nuisance. Respond appropriately and politely, addressing the substance of their complaint or post rather than getting emotionally involved. Be consistent, and keep an issue log – a document that keeps a note of all of the things that have happened in the past and how they have been dealt with. While I'm usually in favour of answering and engaging everyone on a Facebook page there comes a time when it's best to say nothing – your other readers will recognize the troll and will not blame you in the slightest for not responding. Don't take anything personally; the troll is usually having a go at the entity – the 'library' or the organization itself – rather than at an individual. Finally, if all else fails, a tough line needs to be taken; if a troll makes personal comments about a member of staff it may actually be best to delete the post and to ban the member. However, you need to be upfront about this, which also gives you an opportunity to post an explanatory article that explains what your policies are regarding posting to your page. Don't be afraid to act 'tough'; your fans will actually appreciate it.

LinkedIn

We have already looked briefly at LinkedIn in Chapter 2, and I'd like to return to the tool once again, because it's a great tool to use when communicating. It describes itself on the website at www.linkedin.com as the 'world's largest professional network' and it has over 300 million users, having been launched in 2003. Many people regard the resource as the place to promote yourself and to get your CV or resumé out to a potential employer, but it would do the service an injustice to leave it at that. In truth, it's an excellent communication tool; not only can you message friends and colleagues, or ask them to pass on a message to a third party, but you can join various groups. It's for this purpose that I think it's worth exploring, since there are over 2 million LinkedIn groups with 8000 new ones created each week (http://expandedramblings.com/index.php/by-the-numbers-a-few-important-linkedin-stats/8/#.VBh1ZqN-t1M). Consequently there are bound to be a few groups that will be of interest to you. They might cover particular subject areas, such as digital libraries or professional networks. There are groups that support conferences or organizations, and groups for fans of everything from beer to football teams and beyond. Of course, if there isn't a group that covers your interest you can always create one for yourself, for your library community or for colleagues.

Although this is purely a personal observation, I generally find that the discussions in LinkedIn groups tend to be of a higher calibre than those I find on traditional newsgroups or mailing lists. If I need to get advice, have a question answered or have a good discussion, LinkedIn groups are one of the places that I'll think of going first. Of course, if I can also help someone else out, I'll happily do so as well.

LinkedIn also allows for the creation of pages for different organizations, such as The British Library, and it's helpful to be able to use the service to discover if you are connected with anyone in an organization, either directly or with 'second degree' connections. You can follow specific organizations and be kept up to date with their posts, adding in your own comments as appropriate.

Google+ communities

It will come as very little surprise to know that the Google+ social network also has a communities option (https://plus.google.com/communities), which works in a very similar way. You can join groups which cover every conceivable subject area from the serious to the ridiculous, and, once again, if you can't find a group to join, you can create your own. I have created a UK Library community at http://bit.ly/Xd7nXe, and librarians and like-minded people can post information about events and news items, ask questions, link to videos or websites, and so on.

They are a great way to keep up to date with whatever is going on in your area of interest, and they're especially useful if you're very active on the Google+ network. The use of hangouts, for example, can provide a real sense of community and cohesion that you don't get with any other resource. On the other hand, there are only so many hours in the day, so you may need to make a choice between Google+ communities and LinkedIn groups. I would certainly recommend exploring both to see which supports your activities and interests most closely.

Blogging

A blog is a good way to communicate with members, clients and colleagues. Blogging is a very early form of social communication and interaction, since it first started back in the late 1990s, but it is still very popular. The leading blogging platform in the USA is Blogger (www.blogger.com) which has over 46 million unique visitors each month. Almost 7 million people blog on blog platforms, while another 12 million use social networks to share their thoughts and ideas. Companies that use blogs have 97% more inbound links, and they are widely used by consumers when making a purchasing decision (statistics from www.social4retail.com/the-blog-economy-blogging-stats-infographic-2014.html). Gone are the days when blogs all used to look like diaries; some very popular websites are actually blogs, such as the Huffington Post (www.huffingtonpost.co.uk), Mashable (http://mashable.com) and TechCrunch (http://techcrunch.com).

A blog allows for a different type of communication from those previously mentioned. The website is good for authoritative content and facts and figures. Twitter is the 'go-to' tool for brief message shots, while Facebook is a good place to share information and show a human side to the library or organization. A blog is a good place to share longer pieces, both with an existing audience, but also to attract new readers into your conversations. In order to get readers in the first instance, there are a number of things that you need to take into account when writing blog posts. Posts need to have a compelling title; if you are tweeting that you have written a new blog post (and you should!) it's got to capture instant interest. It should therefore be short enough to tweet, using power keywords such as 'hot', 'killer' or 'dynamite'. If you can include a number as well, that will increase the number of readers. Now of course, that's an ideal, and for the majority of us one that is almost unachievable or inappropriate for the content that we're sharing, but 'shorter and with keywords' is always worth remembering.

We're communicating in a social environment now, so it's worth including some social media buttons that allow people to re-share your material on Facebook, Twitter, LinkedIn and so on. Key search engines will also find and index your blog posts (in my personal experience I can write a blog post and be able to find it on Google Blogsearch inside 20 minutes), so you need to optimize for them as well. So again the title is important, any headings should include keywords, and repeat keywords during the post. Any images that you use should be Pinterest-friendly, with a 'Pin It' button for ease of sharing (see p. 133). It's worthwhile putting some effort into the blog as blogs that have daily content added will get five times more traffic than those which only post weekly or less often. However, there's no point in starting off with overly ambitious targets, since that's just setting yourself up for a fall. Create a calendar and decide when to blog; as with Facebook, it's worth getting other authors involved, so ask other members of your team, or colleagues from other departments or sections, to consider writing a guest blog now and then. The blog posts that you write should also be longer than other forms of social media engagement; 1500 words or more is a good figure to aim for. There are a few other oddities when it comes to blogging – they get the highest traffic on a Monday morning, and posts published on Thursdays get more social shares than on any other day, so if you can only manage to post twice a week, those are good days to aim for.

I often hear the exasperated question 'But what do I blog about?' and it's a fair point. I would certainly start by looking at what other similar libraries or organizations are covering, just to get some idea. Obviously I can't help on the actual content, because each blog should be different, but there are a few types of post that I would suggest you consider.

Informative

You are an expert in your own field (I know you probably doubt that, but really, you are!) and other people want to learn from people who know more than they do – especially from those they can relate to. Given your role as a librarian or information professional, that immediately places you into a position of trust. Keep an eye open for what is happening in your world of news; is there an event happening that you can provide information on? Can you make some useful comments on the way that the Chancellor's Budget statement affects your subject area? Has the President recently signed something into law which your readers need to know about? Has there been a change in the rules and regulations of something which makes a dramatic difference to a key segment of your industry? Not only will people be looking to the library for that type of information, so you should be researching it anyway, but people will also be looking online as well, and if you are able to post quickly there is a greater chance that your post will be picked up early and shared more than those that come later.

Teaching

If you can provide a quick training tip every now and then, people will bookmark your blog, tweet your hints and will come back for more. 'Five killer Google Search hints' may sound slightly dramatic, but aren't you already keen to know what they are? Blog posts that I write which update people on search functionality are always well read and shared. People are always looking online for the ways to do something – that's one of the reasons that YouTube is so popular, after all! Never underestimate your own skillset; what you can do with ease other people may well struggle over, and the more that you can share and assist people, the more they will want to come back and read more.

Create lists

My 'Five killer Google Search hints' suggestion in the previous paragraph is a good example of this. People really do seem to like to have numbered lists; they're fun to read and they present information in bite-sized chunks, which is generally appreciated.

Review things

I spend a lot of time on my blog reviewing search engines. It's a quick and easy way to create a post, because the product is doing most of the work for you. In my case I will check to see what the search engine covers, what search functionality it has, whether it has help screens, what the results page looks like, and so on. It's unlikely that you'll also be reviewing search engines, but it's a simple matter to do something similar for other gadgets, cars, magazines – almost anything! It also helps if you can refer back to previous blog posts, which allow people to compare and contrast your reviews.

Opinion pieces

These are perhaps slightly more contentious, because you may not be employed by your organization to hand out opinions willy-nilly. However, this is where it may well be a good time to ask someone else in your organization to provide their thoughts on and insights into an issue. People do generally understand that blogs are often written through the eyes of a particular individual, so they will expect a certain amount of bias and so be upfront about it. It's also worthwhile linking back to other blogs or news items that share the same, or ideally opposing, viewpoints, since that offers a more comprehensive approach.

Links

Almost every post that I write links to something else. The blog either contains a link to the search engine, social media tool or news item, or will link to something that does link on further – such as an initial link to someone else's blog post. If I need to know what's going on in the world, I'll very often start by searching blogs, to see if someone has talked about something, but most particularly to find a link to an original source that I can then use myself.

Multimedia pieces

Remember that blog postings do not need to simply be a collection of words put together in a pleasing fashion. They can include screenshots, photographs or video. The Information Literacy Weblog, at http://information-literacy.blogspot.co.uk, always contains at least one image; sometimes it's related to the blog itself, but at other times it's an attractive image from nature, for example. It may not add any informative content to the blog, but it does draw the eye in and provide a smile for the reader, which is never a bad thing.

Request posts

Ask for people's ideas and opinions on things. This might be a counterpoint to the 'Five killer tips' type of post – ask people to share their ideas and thoughts in the comments section of the blog. Not only will you learn something useful yourself, it encourages people to return to the post to see what other people have said. You could also include quizzes or polls in this category as well; there are plenty of tools that are freely available that allow you to create these with no programming knowledge at all – simply cut and paste the code into the blog post and you are ready to go.

Organizational news

If your organization is moving, the library is changing, or you have a new CEO, that's information which is worth sharing. Take and share photographs of before and after the move, or see if you can get an interview with the new CEO to share her ideas with readers.

Re-use other social media pieces

If you have done something interesting elsewhere on social media, you want to share that as widely as you can. If you are creating a collection of images on Pinterest, for example, that's a good blog post there and then, particularly because you can link to your Pinterest account. Alternatively, if there's an interesting discussion on your Facebook page, ask for thoughts and ideas in a blog post to cross-fertilize your readership's responses.

Humorous and light-hearted material

I wouldn't suggest making a habit of posts of this nature, but one every now and then does help to show the human side of the library staff. No one will complain about a fun post at Christmas time, for example, or a summer holiday post on 'Five great books to read on holiday'.

Chat rooms

Chat rooms do exactly what you would expect of them – they are a place to sit and chat with other people – usually by text, but sometimes visually as well. We've already previously discussed Google+ Hangouts (see p. 78), so I don't intend to go into those again. It's just worth a quick reminder, however, that they are available, and there's no reason why you shouldn't use one to run one-on-one or several communication sessions for Q&A, specialized interview sessions, and so on. Facebook also has a video option linked to the message element, so you could also use that as a way of connecting directly with your members or patrons. If you're still keen on the idea of video chat, but don't want to get involved with the two major players, it is worth taking a look at Appear In, which you can find at https://appear.in. You can create a room, call it whatever you like and invite people to join you. You are limited to a total of eight participants, and if you have webcams you'll be able to see each other as well as hear everyone. It's also possible to claim a room by registering your e-mail address, and you can then create custom backgrounds, give people 'keys' to the room (thereby controlling who can enter) and kick people out if necessary.

'Ask a Librarian' services are already very popular, with large numbers of academic libraries offering the service, as well as some public or national libraries. Cardiff University, for example, offers a live chat service between the hours of 9 a.m. and 5 p.m. Monday to Friday.

A lot of software packages are available that an aspiring chatter can use in order to get the conversations off the ground and flowing. Chatzy (www.chatzy.com) is a very good example. It's a free tool, and you don't have to register to use it. Simply visit the site, fill out the basic form (name, title of the chat and so on) and then enter the room. Alternatively, if you want something a little more secure you can use one of their virtual rooms, to which you can limit access, control what people do (such as embed YouTube videos), create room admins, and so on. Chatzy will host the chat room for you, or if you prefer you can pay for a premium account to embed the chat room on your blog or website. chatWING, at http://chatwing.com, also offers numerous options to customize your own chat room, and it can be used across different devices such as desktop browsers, smartphones or tablets. You can create a room and save it; my room is at http://chatwing.com/philbsroom, for example, and you're welcome to go and visit it, though since I don't really publicize it I can't promise that it will be a particularly exciting experience.

Wikis

A wiki is a tool that allows people to create web pages, and add, edit or delete the content that's on them. The pages are usually created using a very simplified markup language, similar to that of a word processor, and the entire collection of pages is usually hosted by the publisher of the wiki software. Wikis differ from blogs in that there is usually more than one author, they are based around pages of subject matter rather than arranged chronologically, and the exact structure is the result of the requirements of the users. Wikis can be public, private, or public to view but limited in the number of people who can author content.

The Wikipedia (http://en.wikipedia.org) is the best known example of a wiki but there are plenty of others. There is the LIS Wiki, the library and information science wiki, at http://liswiki.org/wiki/Main_Page, which was started in 2005 and has over 1400 pages so far. Anyone who has an interest in the subject will find something helpful on the site – articles of interest include cell phones in libraries, vanity publishing, laptop check-outs, consortia and RFID. There is also the Library Success: a Best Practices Wiki, at www.libsuccess.org/Main_Page, which was created to be a 'one stop shop for great ideas and information for all types of librarians'.

As a communication tool, wikis can be very helpful indeed. Users can create pages and links between them quickly and easily, embed images and videos and rearrange content, and they support knowledge sharing. They are a great starting place for putting information together, discussing ideas, and so on, but because they can be changed very quickly they are probably not the best place to put information that you may want to cite at some later stage. They are also best used to serve a very specific purpose and then, unless there is a particularly compelling reason to keep them alive on the web, they should be closed down. When searching for wikis you do find huge numbers that obviously haven't been updated for many years, and this just becomes an encumbrance when searching. However, if a wiki is maintained regularly by a dedicated group, it can be a very useful tool indeed.

There are many different software packages available to create wikis, with many of them running directly on the web in the browser, rather than requiring you to download anything. An excellent site to use in order to find the package that works best for you is the WikiMatrix, which is a comparison site listing dozens of packages, at www.wikimatrix.org, (although this is somewhat out of date now – see the comment in my previous paragraph!).

Sticky note software

Another type of tool that can be used to great effect when communicating with a group of people is to use sticky note software. If you imagine for a moment that you're a trainer, and you want people to tell you what they want to get out of the training session, you could give them each a Post-it note to write on. The notes could then be stuck up on the wall and then rearranged to group similar ideas together. That's essentially what sticky note software does; you can create a 'digital wall' and either allow anyone to access it and post content, or password-access it instead. Users simply double-click on the board, write what they want to say, or upload a file, link to a web page or embed a video and then the owner of the board can move the notes around as necessary, rather like a brainstorming session in fact.

They're a great way to work within an education and training environment. I was working with some teachers, one of whom was about to go into a sex education class; she immediately used the idea of sticky notes to encourage her teenagers to post onto the wall all of the questions they were too embarrassed to ask, which she was then able to work with. Apparently it was the most effective session of that sort that she'd ever run!

However, their value goes beyond that of simply training. As I mentioned, you can use them for brainstorming sessions, for feedback or suggestions, making announcements or keeping and sharing notes either synchronously or asynchronously, as appropriate. They are an excellent arena for allowing people to summarize their thoughts, to adapt ideas based on the sticky notes, or as a guiding tool.

There are, as you would expect, many different packages that you can use, but my personal favourite is Padlet (which used to be called Wallwisher), at http://padlet.com. It's a free resource and very simple to use; you can have a wall up and running inside two minutes. There's an example of one that I created to allow delegates to display their work in Figure 7.2.

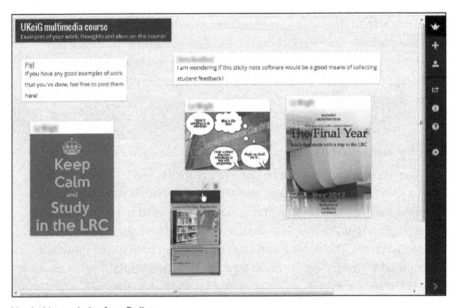

Used with permission from Padlet

Figure 7.2 A Padlet wall in action

However, if you'd prefer to look around a little further and try out other packages I'd suggest taking a look at lino (http://en.linoit.com) – 'sticky and photo sharing for you' – Listhings (http://listhings.com) – 'take sticky notes online' – or Stormboard (https://www.stormboard.com) – 'online brainstorming and collaboration'.

Google Docs

One tool that does deserve its own section is Google Docs, which is a free office suite based on the web. Users can create and edit documents while online, and they can simultaneously collaborate with other users at the same time. This means that you can write a document, or start brainstorming some ideas, and allow other people to work with you at the same time, filling in different sections of the document, correcting errors in others, embedding and hyperlinking. There are three different applications available – Docs, Sheets, and Slides – which can be used on the web, as apps for Chrome which can work offline and also as mobile apps for Android and iOS machines.

All of the files that are created on Google Drive, although they can be downloaded and edited separately; they are compatible with Microsoft Office file formats. The advantages of the tools are that they are simple and easy to use without the complexity that you find with other office suites, storage is simple, they can be shared widely with other people and they integrate into other Google products, such as Google+. However, it is necessary to have a Google account in order to create them, which of course is the whole purpose as far as Google is concerned; it wants to get users tightly integrated to its different services so that they are less likely to migrate elsewhere.

Distributing your content

Once you have created content you're going to want to share it with other people. In some instances this is just part and parcel of using a particular tool – you distribute your content in a wiki simply by writing it, and your thoughts or comments on a sticky note wall are there for your fellow collaborators to view. Failing that you may decide to send your work via e-mail, but there are often size limitations that restrict what you can do.

However, there are plenty of tools that you can use to put your material into the cloud and then share with other people. A good example here is Dropbox, at www.dropbox.com, which is a free service that you can use to archive, store and share your content, either just with yourself or with colleagues. When you create an account the service creates a folder on your system and if you save a file of any description into the Dropbox folder it automatically gets copied onto the server where it can be shared. If you use multiple devices it can sync to all of those as well, so you always have access to your material wherever you are.

Summary

One could of course argue that any transaction across social media is communication of one sort or another, and I wouldn't disagree with that at all. However, there are some tools, as we have seen, that are primarily designed to share ideas back and forth, to allow us to interact and ask and answer questions. There are many different types of communication, from the short question and answer to discussions and longer 'thought pieces'. Many tools are available for this purpose, but I have covered some of the main ones in this chapter. While you don't have to engage with your clients and patrons by using all of them, it certainly makes sense to consider the activity – 'communication' – and decide which of them most support what you are trying to say, and who you want to communicate with.

URLs mentioned in this chapter

Appear In https://appear.in

Blogger www.blogger.com

chatWING http://chatwing.com

■   Author's room at chatWING http://chatwing.com/philbsroom

Chatzy www.chatzy.com

Dropbox www.dropbox.com

Facebook https://en.gb.facebook.com

■   **Cheshire Public Libraries Facebook page** https://www.facebook.com/cheshirelibrary/posts/10152514300455513:0

■   **Essex Libraries Facebook page** https://www.facebook.com/EssexLibraries

Google+ communities https://plus.google.com/communities

■   UK Library community http://bit.ly/Xd7nXe

Hootsuite https://hootsuite.com

Huffington Post www.huffingtonpost.co.uk

Information Literacy Weblog http://information-literacy.blogspot.co.uk

Library Success: a Best Practices Wiki www.libsuccess.org/Main_Page

LinkedIn www.linkedin.com

lino http://en.linoit.com

LIS Wiki http://liswiki.org/wiki/Main_Page

Listhings http://listhings.com

Mashable http://mashable.com

Padlet http://padlet.com
SocialMention* www.socialmention.com
Stormboard https://www.stormboard.com
TechCrunch http://techcrunch.com
Topsy www.topsy.com
Tweetdeck https://tweetdeck.twitter.com
Tweriod www.tweriod.com
Twitter – list of library Twitter accounts
    https://twitter.com/Philbradley/lists/libraries
We Follow www.wefollow.com
WikiMatrix www.wikimatrix.org
Wikipedia http://en.wikipedia.org

 Visit the Facet Publishing YouTube channel
(www.youtube.com/user/facetpublishing) for Phil Bradley's video
A guide to advanced Twitter use.

CHAPTER 8

Marketing and promotion – the groundwork

Introduction

If you ever do a word association quiz with someone and say the word
'library' they are probably going to come back with either 'books' or
'reading'. No real surprise of course, but those of us who work in the
information industry know just how very far off the mark those
associations are now. Step into any library and you'll see computers, Wi-Fi
access, information on e-books and e-magazines, training sessions on how
to get the best out of the internet, and so on. Unfortunately, as a profession
we are often accused (rightly so in my opinion) of keeping too quiet about
what we do and the facilities that are available for our members and
patrons. Social media gives us a real opportunity to change this for the
better, if we are prepared to come out from behind the desks and go to
where the conversations are. As bears repetition, Stephen Abram put it
very well when he said 'Outside the library is still the library'. We cannot
expect people to come into the library – to ask us questions, to borrow
books or to find resources that they need – when they can ask those same
questions on Twitter or discuss them with their friends on Facebook.

Blending your social media presences

If you take a random selection of libraries – be they academic, public or
corporate – and see how they are represented on social media you will
probably be struck by one really important point. That is, that some
libraries will have a great Facebook page, with lots of likes and
conversations, and virtually no Twitter presence. Alternatively, they may be

really busy pinning images on Pinterest and be doing very little on LinkedIn, and so on. One of the dangers of social media is that it's far too easy to view it in terms of the tools themselves. Clients sometimes ask me to set up a Twitter account for them, and teach them how to use it, but when I ask the question 'Why do you actually want a Twitter account?' they are left puzzled, and fall back on the line 'because everyone else has one'. If you view these tools in that manner your journey into using social media has stalled at the first hurdle. As I have said previously and make no excuse for saying again, you have to focus on the activities first, and then the tools will follow. As we have already seen, social media tools can be used in a variety of different ways, but unless you blend their use together and they support what you want to achieve, the most that you can expect to have is a half-hearted and meagre result.

When you wish to promote or market the information service, that is the activity, and you need to decide not only which tools to use in order to achieve your aim, but how to use them together. For example, if you write a blog post, you need to promote that blog post by tweeting a link to it, with a catchy line. If you have put something on your website, add a link to it on Facebook. You shouldn't just do one thing with your social media work – it has to work much harder than that. For example, when I write a blog post, a tweet links to it automatically within the hour. Because I have then tweeted a link, that (also automatically) gets added to my Delicious bookmarking account. That link in turn ends up on the home page of my website where all my visitors can get to see it. With one activity (writing the blog) I'm actually able to do three other things at the same time with no additional work on my part. This is something that I point out when people say to me that they don't have time to get involved with social media. We all only have 24 hours in the day, but it's how we use them that makes the difference. If you look at Twitter as just another thing that you need to do during your 9–5 work day, of course it will look daunting, and the temptation is to put off doing it. However, if you regard Twitter as a tool that helps you communicate and converse or promote and market your library then you can incorporate it into your daily routine as part of those activities. Of course, something else will have to give and I fully accept that, but to paraphrase Anthony Robbins, 'If you only do what you've always done, you'll only have what you've already got.'

It's also important to remember that different tools should be used in different ways. While both Twitter and blogs are good for communication, they are for different types of communication – short and snappy or longer, more thoughtful pieces. One temptation is to provide exactly the same information in different formats – but followers don't want to see the same message on Twitter that they have just read on Facebook, for example.

A consistent approach is extremely valuable. Ideally try and use exactly the same name across different platforms; that makes it much easier for people to recognize who you are, and far easier to search for. This isn't always possible of course, and certainly on Twitter many names and variations thereof have already been taken, so you may need to do some research before making a choice. If you have members of staff posting on behalf of the library or organization it makes sense to ensure that the library's name is included in their 'handle'; not only does it make it clear that it's not their personal viewpoints, but it also means that if they decide to leave your employ they can't take 'your' followers with them into another position with another organization. Of course, there is nothing to stop you having a single name and letting staff share the password so that they are posting with one voice, as it were – as long as it's consistent! I would also suggest that you use exactly the same avatar (a visual representation of your social media name or account) whenever possible. People very quickly come to recognize and remember an image, and when skimming through a collection of tweets or postings something which is bright and memorable will encourage them to pause for the few moments it takes to read your words of wisdom.

Your avatar should correspond to the type of account that you intend to create. If you are creating a social media presence for the organization it makes sense to use an already recognized logo. However, if the logo is too complicated (such as a university crest, for example) then it may well become a simple mish-mash of colours when reduced in size and used on Twitter. The audience that you intend to obtain should be able to connect with the avatar, so if you're working with young people you may find that something bright works best, while a photograph of you in a suit may be more appropriate if you are dealing with business professionals. If you are going to use a photograph of yourself try and keep it head and shoulders, since a full or half-length image is again going to be so small it could be almost anybody. There are various theories about looking towards or away from the camera; I prefer looking directly at the camera, but the main point is to feel comfortable – don't forget that social media is inherently informal. If you choose to use something that's rather more abstract try and link it in some way to what you or your organization does: perhaps an image of a stethoscope if it's a health library, or a suitcase if you're writing about travel-related issues. Your avatar is going to be seen around the world, so make sure that it's not offensive to other people or cultures; it seems to be an obvious point but other cultures' mores are not always obvious. There may be times when you want to be associated with a particular event or campaign that's taking place – particularly on Twitter –and you can add what is generally referred to as a

Figure 8.1
The author's Twitter avatar with associated 'twibbons'

'twibbon' to your image. This is usually in the form of a small icon and you may wish to leave enough space in your avatar to allow the addition without disguising who you are! As you can see from Figure 8.1, I have got three twibbons on my Twitter avatar; one for my favourite football team, one for CILIP, the Chartered Institute of Library and Information Professionals, and one supporting National Libraries Day. If you're interested in the idea of twibbons, you can visit the site at http://twibbon.com/.

One crucial point, however, is that whatever you do, you should change away from the default that is created when you first start an account. All that does is mark you out as a complete novice who hasn't taken time to work out what to do, and as a result it's likely that you won't be taken seriously. A few other don'ts when it comes to avatars: please don't use a pet photograph, unless of course you're creating a social media account for your pet (don't laugh, it happens all the time!), since most people would prefer to have discussions with a real person. It's not a good idea to add a picture of you and your partner unless it really is a shared personal account because again, it's helpful to know exactly who you are talking to. Many people use cartoon avatars, which is fine if it's for a personal account, but it doesn't look very professional in a work environment. Don't use pictures of yourself from your past or from when you were a baby for the same reason. Finally don't use any photographs of yourself in a state of undress or doing anything inappropriate such as being drunk. You would think it shouldn't be necessary to point these out, but most of us have seen at least one memorable example of this over the years. Now I realize that I have probably offended a fair number of my own contacts with this list, so I should best add that there are always excellent and well thought-out exceptions to the above rules of thumb!

Getting past the organization roadblock

One problem that I can unfortunately promise that you'll come across very quickly in your efforts to use social media is that the 'powers that be' will in all likelihood be less than enthusiastic. They will probably put barriers in your way along the lines of 'we don't do it this way', 'Facebook is for kids', 'there are too many technical issues' or 'it's not your job'. The last one, by the way, is one that I hear most often from librarians who I talk to, and it's one of the most irritating – if it's not the information professional's job to market and promote information and their information centre, I do wonder whose job it is.

Misunderstanding of social media

A lot of these concerns are based on fear and misunderstanding, and in order to overcome them you first have to understand them. People are afraid that if their organization uses social media they will experience some catastrophic disaster that will make them look stupid. It's certainly true that there have been some amazing disasters as a result of using social media (see the Appendix, p. 159), but the main disaster is when people don't react quickly and effectively to the error that's been made. Rather than planning for the error in advance and having set action points, their answer seems to be not to get involved in the first place, which is a far bigger and more serious error. It's like not sending a liner out to sea because you're afraid it might sink instead of ensuring that it has enough lifeboats and running regular drills. This fear also comes from a feeling of misplaced control; managers usually like to control things, but social media doesn't work that way – in fact quite the opposite. If someone wants to engage with an organization they can do so if there's a social media presence, but if there isn't, they may well just decide to go onto Twitter, Facebook or any of the other platforms and make their points that way. By not having an involvement with these platforms the library staff are being placed in a position where they can't respond. To use social media is to interact with people; keep the website for the information that needs to be broadcast to everyone.

In order to overcome that fear, I'm tempted to say that you should try and replace it with another, even bigger one, along the lines of 'social media is like the internet; you were afraid that the internet would be detrimental to us, but not to have it now is what would be detrimental', but I'm not overly keen on the idea of scare tactics. Rather, you want to point out which other libraries are doing things on Twitter or Facebook, and you're not going to have to go very far to get some good examples that are appropriate to you. You may wish to make the point that 'if they are doing it, why aren't we?' but I think the best approach is to admit that there may be mistakes along the way but it's not making mistakes that is important, it's how you recover from them. A good social media policy is a great way forward here, and I'll talk about this later in Chapter 10.

Misunderstanding comes not from using tools, but from listening to what other people, and the mainstream media in particular, say about them. The mainstream media is not interested in talking about how useful social media is, how much time it can save, and how much more effectively you can do your job – where is the story in that? What's much more interesting is to talk about the teenager whose friends wrecked the house while her parents were away by widely advertising a party on Facebook, resulting in hundreds of people turning up. Stories about how Twitter can be used to bully other people, or Facebook allowing hate groups to create pages, are far more interesting and sensational than the story about how the library staff advertised an event and doubled the number of people who usually turned up, or increased readership of their blog post by a third. A common complaint about Facebook is 'My teenage children use that all of the time; how can that possibly be a good tool for us to use?' and for Twitter the criticism is often 'We can't use anything that's got such a stupid name!'

Opposition from other departments

You may also find that some departments in your organization are worried about using social media because they think that their own jobs are at risk, and that is a legitimate concern. We're all used to the refrain of 'Why do we need librarians now we have the internet and Google?' and press and communications departments will similarly wonder if they have a future when communicating is now so simple and easy, and a single tweet can reach a market much bigger than they could ever conceive of. Technical support departments – all too often used as an IT police force – worry that they're not going to be able to control the resources that people are using, leading to security breaches, rampant viruses running like wildfire through the network, and so on. Managers are concerned that their staff are going to spend all day playing Farmville on Facebook and not doing their work, which in turn will reflect badly on them.

Focus on benefits

The answer to all of these considerations is first to acknowledge them and accept that people are scared. Rather than talk about social media, or even the tools that you want to use, refocus the discussion on the activities that you or they can do better. Your communications staff will have a greater variety of platforms on which to serve their message, and better ways to communicate directly with members or interested parties. Your technical support staff will be able to more easily access machines from a distance to work out what a particular problem is, and so on.

Let the benefits of the situation run the conversation for you. We are now in a period of huge expansion of services on the internet, with more information being made available on a daily basis than we're even able to comprehend. You are going to be in a position to market and promote your library more widely to a global audience than you have ever been able to do before. People from countries that you've never even heard of will be able to subscribe to what you're doing, and will be able to use your work as examples of good practice, and they will in turn be promoting what you are doing. For example, I subscribe to the Facebook page of Cheshire Public Library, which is based in Connecticut; I'll never go to Connecticut and will never visit the library in person, but I really enjoy following their Facebook page because it always has interesting things on it, irrespective of the fact that I'm not in their target demographic. If possible, avoid using the term 'social media', which comes with so much baggage associated with it, as previously mentioned, and take the conversation in the direction of 'We can do xyz more quickly, more effectively and more cheaply with this tool that I've just discovered'. It then becomes rather more difficult to argue against using a tool, because the focus is on the benefits.

Refer to other libraries' practice

It's worth preparing a case for using social media by looking at what other libraries are doing in the area that you are intending to move into. A really powerful phrase which I often see stated in advertising either explicitly or by implication is 'people like you' in order to get agreement on an issue; a sign I saw on a motorway the other day said 'Don't drop litter, other people don't'. The fact is that more and more librarians and libraries are using social media for a variety of purposes, and you want to make it clear that not using these tools and getting involved with the activities that are important to you should be seen as the exception, rather than the rule. 'Libraries like ours' or 'other academic librarians' or 'most other law firms' are certainly phrases that are worth dropping into the conversation with the 'powers that be'. When I'm teaching social media activities and tools one of the questions that I'm often asked is 'Which other libraries are using this tool?' and I fully understand why they're asking – after all, no one wants to be the first to take a risk on something. However, if you're thinking the same thing, I would invite you to look at it in a different manner. It may be true that no other librarian is using that particular tool, but there are plenty who are doing the same activity which that tool is supporting. So in fact, the risk isn't that great, particularly since in most cases the tools that you want to try out are not paid for and you can always have a free trial, even if it is a commercial product. If the tool works, all well and good, and you should consider continuing its use. However, if the tool doesn't do what you want, then you have learned a valuable lesson. You can then blog about what the tool did or didn't do, and use the experience as professional updating which you can share with your colleagues in other libraries. In the 'old days' making a mistake was a big deal because products cost hundreds if not thousands of pounds. That's not how things work now and you should not be hamstrung by past experiences. After all, if you don't make mistakes you're not learning anything, and if you're not learning anything you're standing still at best, or going backwards rapidly.

Promotion and marketing also needs to be considered from the time viewpoint. The rise of Twitter, LinkedIn and Facebook has really caused us to review what 'new' means. In years gone by something that was news could have happened a few hours ago, or even the day before. However, since people can blog and tweet so quickly, 'new' could be something that happened a few seconds ago. Indeed, while there is disagreement on the half-life of a tweet (some say that it's as little as 5 minutes, others say 18 minutes while others say 2.8 hours) there's general agreement that it's not long. Consequently if you are promoting or marketing the library or a particular event, it's got to be done quickly, because traditional methods really don't work any longer and, besides, people are not going to be looking for things in traditional places any longer. Speed is of the essence, because that's what people expect, so promotion and discussions have to happen in a timely manner, and while I dislike being proscriptive this simply cannot be done without using tools such as Twitter, LinkedIn and Facebook.

Fitting appropriate content to platforms

Your content needs to fit the different platforms that you intend using. Twitter will give the highlights, Facebook allows you to go into a little more depth, LinkedIn will give you the opportunity of discussing something with experts, Google+ postings will help when it comes to getting rankings with their search engine, Pinterest will be a helpful tool when it comes to any imagery that you can associate with the activity, Flickr is a great way to allow other people to share their images of whatever the event happens to be, and so on. Each of those platforms will appeal to different people, and while it's tempting to simply copy the same information all of the way across the platforms it may not always be the best way to get the message across. Not only does the message need to fit the platform, it also needs to fit the audience; the people on LinkedIn are unlikely to be the same ones that are on Facebook, for example. For example, a tweet about a public library 'rhyme time' session will in all probability be more effective than a post about it on LinkedIn, but a blog about how the event was planned and executed may be particularly valuable to other librarians who are thinking of doing something similar.

Return on investment

Your ROI, or return on investment, is also something that you'll need to consider when it comes to marketing and promotion. Erik Qualman in his book on Socialnomics (www.socialnomics.net) put it bluntly when he said 'The ROI of social media is that your business will be around in the next five years.' Social media is here to stay – it's not some flash in the pan fad, and we have to work with it; even if you try and ignore social media, that's still a relationship! I see the same kind of objections to social media that I saw to the internet 20, even 10 years ago. Libraries (or more particularly their parent body) simply didn't see the value in having websites, because they were used to people finding them in the yellow pages, the telephone directory or through articles in the press. Now, however, people expect to find that a search for a library website will turn up a library website. They expect to be able to find your contact details or directions on how to find you via the website. Not having a website is virtually unthinkable. Even though we're still at a very early stage with social media we ignore it at our peril, but that's often a difficult point to get across, particularly to the boss who wants to know exactly what the ROI is.

You could, of course, argue that it's difficult to see the ROI on having telephones, or in employees telling other people about their brand, but that's really quite a negative approach to take. You can measure ROI on social media by an increase in the number of people who are following you, responding to you and copying your message onwards on different social media platforms. You can run analytics on visitors to the website or to blog posts to see where they come from, and you can provide statistics on the number of Facebook likes or Google+ +1s that you get over a period of time. There are also online tools that you can use, such as Klout (https://klout.com), which helps you measure your 'Klout score' to see how popular your brand is across social media. Although those are really rather brutal measurements, they can be helpful. What's more useful, though, is to talk about the rather more imponderable results that you can get: better relationships with people, more involvement with the library or brand, or people reposting your information onto others. In short, you want more people to perceive that you (either individually, or as a representative of the library or the organization) are skilled and expert in your particular area. People address questions to people that they know, but in most instances we can expect to find them asking those questions on social media, rather than physically coming into the library. If we are able to (and here's that phrase again) go to where the conversations are, so that we can quickly and informatively engage with users, members or patrons, that's some of the very best marketing that you can possibly do. Conversely, by not being there you're also making a very strong negative statement about your skills, expertise and interest in your audience. The more that people can see how helpful you are on Facebook or Twitter, the more often they will come back, engage with you and suggest that others do the same. Remember, this is all about the engagement process.

You are involved in conversations on social media; you can leave the broadcast messages to your traditional websites or forms of communication. A printed newsletter might be a great way to communicate with one segment of your market, but it will be an increasingly small one, and more importantly, one that can't engage with you.

The messages that you send out to people, and the conversations that you want to have with them, also need to focus on what they are going to get out of it. There isn't much point writing a Facebook status update explaining that there will be a makerspace event at a library over the weekend. [If you're unfamiliar with the term a makerspace is simply a community space with tools of one type or another. Within a library context this might be a situation in which librarians collaborate with other people to share expertise, tools and an educational environment to encourage hands-on learning.] You need to focus on the reasons why they want to attend: so that they can learn about 3D printing for example, or that they could bring along a broken gadget and see if it could be fixed, or give their children the opportunity to explore some new apps on a tablet. Your reason for having the event might be to interact more with the community, or to get more people through the doors, or to get the press to come along, but no one will turn up if you attempt to use those as compelling reasons to attend.

Search engine optimization (SEO)

Search engine optimization is also an important thing to consider when looking to market or promote your services, because as well as getting to the people who already know about you, you want to get to those who don't. It's the cyber equivalent of a drive-by; someone looking online for something interesting to do at the weekend, or who is searching for more information about their particular interest. SEO is basically trying to ensure that your content, be it a website, web page, tweet or blog post gets a good ranking in the search engine(s) of choice, therefore increasing profile, presence and ultimately engagement. There are several sets of magic numbers when it comes to using social media posts, and it's worthwhile being aware of them. A tweet needs to be shorter than the 140 characters, not only because you want people to retweet it without them having to spend time modifying it, but because people do like short snippets of content. Some of these things you can't have any control over (domain names are particularly attractive and desirable if they are exactly 8 characters long, for example), but others you can. Facebook status posts which are 40 characters yield 86% higher engagement, while 80 characters will give you 66% higher engagement. Google+ headlines work best if they are below 60 characters, to keep them all on the same line, while ideal headlines are only 6 words long. Blog posts which are engaging take about 7 minutes to read, with a total of 1600 words (source: http://socialtimes.com/science-post-length-online-infographic_b146635). Now, I'm certainly not going to suggest that you immediately start becoming paranoid and obsessive about figures like this, and there's no doubt that other experts will have entirely different figures, but what I would say is that writing copy for social media postings can be something of a dark art that takes practice. Monitor what you're doing, and try and figure out what works for you and what doesn't. When you find the 'sweet spot' then you can really start to market your message effectively.

Location

A recent study showed that 20% of the images on Pinterest are in the Food and Drink category. Now, unless you have a particularly impressive cafeteria linked to your library you might not see the particular value of this statistic. However, what it shows is that people like to interact with their surroundings, by taking pictures of their food at a restaurant, for example, tweeting where they are and what they're doing, or using location services on Facebook to tell everyone where they are and who they are with. Tools such as Foursquare, at https://foursquare.com, have been a favourite of people for several years, allowing them to 'check in' to particular places, such as their place of work, local attraction or coffee shop. If they check in often enough they may become 'Mayor' of that particular place, which may result in a free weekly coffee, for example. Users can also discover places that their friends really like, and you can share yours with them.

It's worthwhile spending the few minutes that is necessary to create a check-in option for your library, event or conference so that people have another opportunity to promote your service via their own status updates. Encourage your visitors to check in, and you can create a page of information about it. The Topeka and Shawnee County Public Library have a nice example at http://foursquare.com/venue/308934 which is shown in Figure 8.2.

Pages like this are quick and easy to set up, they require minimal

Used with permission from Topeka and Shawnee County Public Library

Figure 8.2 The Topeka and Shawnee County Public Library
Foursquare entry

maintenance, and once your users get used to the idea that they can check in at the library they are going to do all of the work for you.

Consumer rather than creator

If you still have problems getting access to social media platforms it may be because those annoying 'powers that be' still have a concern over what you or other employees may want to create. Consequently it's worth reminding them that social media offers two sides of the same coin: not only can you create, but you can consume as well. A few quick searches (at home if necessary) should be all that's needed to show them that the library or organization is being mentioned or discussed on Twitter, Facebook and the rest of them. It's only by keeping an eye on these references that you can then respond to them. Indeed, to go one stage further, it's not only the organization that you should be interested in, but other references to your subjects of interest. Run a search on your favourite search engine and see just how many results are not actually results at all, but are simply pointers to social media accounts and references. By not having access to this information you're unable to do your job properly, so focus on the activities (professional updating, current awareness, selective dissemination of information) and the benefits they will bring (up-to-the-minute monitoring at no cost with little extra work on your behalf) rather than getting into a long discussion about how you won't be tempted to use Facebook to talk to your friends!

Monitoring tools

I previously mentioned Klout, which helps you get an indication of perhaps how well you are performing with social media, and it's helpful as a general barometer, but there are other tools that you can use to make monitoring mentions of your library, event or hashtag much easier. Hootsuite (www.hootsuite.com) is helpful, since you can create a column to monitor any search, @name or hashtag for example, but it's only semi-automated, and there are many different things that you might want to monitor. For example:

- the name of your library or organization
- information on your customers – either specific influencers in your sector or something rather broader
- competition – it's unlikely that your library will be in competition with other libraries, but it's quite probable that your organization will be, and you'll want to keep an eye on what they're doing
- the library and science world in general – what new developments are taking place that you need to be kept up to date with? More generally, the subject area that your parent organization works in
- specific keywords or searches – single words are often not enough, and some tools will allow you to create longer, more complex search patterns
- hashtags – you may use a specific hashtag for your library or organization, use one for an event, simply wish to follow a conference or keep watch on a trending issue.

As you would expect, there are plenty of tools that will let you monitor all of these options and plenty more besides. Many of them are commercial offerings, but equally most of them will also allow you to receive a certain number of alerts every month for free, or they will only monitor a small number of terms for you.

Mention (https://web.mention.com) is an e-mail based service, with additional desktop notifications that pop up when it discovers anything new, keeping you absolutely on top of the news. You can create an alert with keywords, a single word or phrase, and you can exclude words from your search. You can also manage your alerts directly from their website by adding your social media accounts (Twitter, Facebook and so on) in real time to share, quote or re-tweet. As such, it's an extremely fast and effective way to share the content that you find.

Talkwalker Alerts, at www.talkwalker.com/alerts, is a very simple and straightforward service to use. You can create an alert using a number of options; the query, results from news, blogs or discussions, how often (daily or weekly), and how many alerts you want. The search will be monitored and every day (or week) you will receive an e-mail with the latest results for you, or you can add them to your favourite RSS reader. It's a service that I use myself and find it very helpful.

Tweetbeep, at http://tweetbeep.com, keeps track of conversations that mention you or your interests with hourly updates. Backtweets (http://backtweets.com) does a similar job, but it also keeps a Twitter archive, so you can view older material as well.

Netvibes, at www.netvibes.com, is a home or start page, but it has very simple and easy to use 'widgets' that can be used to monitor references in social media. These include Twitter, Delicious, Google News, search engine search results, Facebook, Google+ and so on. Once the search has been set up Netvibes will continue to monitor the terms and resources, bringing news back to you on a regular basis, with no further input from you.

There are of course many other tools, particularly social media search engines such as Icerocket (www.icerocket.com), SocialMention* (www.socialmention.com) and Topsy, (www.topsy.com) and the latter two allow for e-mail alerts or links to RSS feeds.

Summary

Marketing and promotion is not a simple task; that's why there are so many companies out there offering to do it for you at vastly inflated costs. However, there's no reason why that needs to be the case, as I have hopefully demonstrated. All that it takes is a clear idea of what you want to achieve, what your goals and parameters are and who your audience is. Once you have that, you can match that to the appropriate tools and start to work. In the next chapter I'll take a look at some of the practical ways in which you can start using tools to get a better presence online and on social media platforms.

URLs mentioned in this chapter

Backtweets http://backtweets.com

Foursquare https://foursquare.com

 ▪ **The Topeka and Shawnee County Public Library at Foursquare**
 http://foursquare.com/venue/308934

Hootsuite www.hootsuite.com

Icerocket www.icerocket.com

Klout https://klout.com

Mention https://web.mention.com

Netvibes www.netvibes.com

SocialMention* www.socialmention.com

Talkwalker Alerts www.talkwalker.com/alerts

Topsy www.topsy.com

Tweetbeep http://tweetbeep.com

twibbon http://twibbon.com

Visit the Facet Publishing YouTube channel (www.youtube.com/user/facetpublishing) for Phil Bradley's video Some examples of great marketing practice in libraries.

CHAPTER 9

Marketing and promotion – the practicalities

Introduction

Having discussed laying the groundwork for marketing and promoting your library service, event or conference, let's next turn to some of the methods that you can use which should hopefully give you a good social media presence. This chapter is very practically based, using lots of different tools that you may find helpful when planning your marketing and promotion. Most of the tools will be free, though some may have a commercial aspect to them that you might want to explore if you have any extra cash available, but the emphasis here is really doing things on a shoestring budget.

Images

As we've seen before, using visual imagery is a great way to get people to sit up and take notice of what you're doing. Unfortunately all too often we use the tools that are readily available to us, such as Microsoft Word clip art, which while it is convenient is not exactly very exciting. I would suggest that an excellent place to start, and to get some inspiration for posters, Facebook pictures, images that you can tweet about and so on is the BigHugeLabs website at http://bighugelabs.com. All that you need to start off with is an image; a photograph that you've got, an illustration from a library database, perhaps, a logo, or failing that an image that has a Creative Commons Licence that allows you to modify images that the original copyright owner is making freely available for this exact purpose. BigHugeLabs has drag-and-drop options allowing you to create magazine

Figure 9.1
An example of a badge created
in BigHugeLabs

covers, movie posters, pop art posters, jigsaws or calendars. You can create photographic cubes that can be cut out and folded, create billboard-type images or wallpaper with monthly calendars for your computer.

To look at just two examples in detail: you can create your own badges, and Figure 9.1 is an example. You could then print these out, laminate them (cheap laminators can be purchased for about £10 these days) and then hand them out to library visitors. Instead of the image saying 'Press', you could edit it to become anything that you like; sculpture, artist, musician, writer, and so on, to focus on famous people in history. If you have events to mark specific things that happened in history, or biographical sections in your library, these could be a great way of promoting the library – especially if you can get people to wear them when they leave. Alternatively you could encourage children by giving them 'library assistant' badges or something similar. There's a whole host of ways that you could use what is essentially a really simple concept.

A second idea is to create trading cards. Figure 9.2 is an example of one of mine that I use on training courses. It

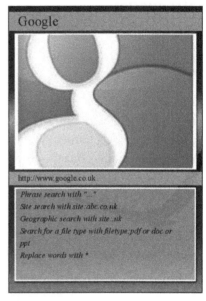

Figure 9.2
A trading card created using
BigHugeLabs

includes the name of a search engine, its URL and then a few search functions. If you create a few of these for different search engines you could leave them next to the computers, hand them out to visitors or use them as aide memoires yourself. Alternatively create a new card every month, based on various themes, events or photographs submitted by users. Children love playing 'Top Trumps', where each card has a photograph of something such as a car, with various criteria below; they try to win cards by choosing one criterion in the hope that it beats the one their opponent has. You could do this for any number of subject areas; start by having a small base set of cards that children can have, and then give them the option of earning new cards every month based on the number of books that they read, for example. I often use trading cards on courses; at the start of the day I give each delegate a collection of the same cards, and they have to interact with other delegates to swap their cards to try and complete an entire set. It's a fun and different way to break the ice.

We're all aware of the 'Keep Calm' posters – you can create your own very easily with the Keepcalm-o-matic website, at www.keepcalm-o-matic. co.uk. You can create a poster that is based on the original bright red 'Keep Calm and Carry On' wartime one, and simply change it to read 'Keep calm and use your library', and these can once again be printed out and laminated, then posted around the campus, the organization or the town. Alternatively you can create variations on a theme by choosing different logos, backgrounds, text colours and fonts. The same site allows you to create a 'thought canvas' where you can choose your words, position them on the poster, choose a background and font size and colour and then print it out. Of course, it goes without saying that with all of these tools you can easily share what you have done across various different social media platforms. Another alternative to more traditional posters is the rather exotically named Pulp-o-mizer, at http://thrilling-tales.webomator.com/ derange-o-lab/pulp-o-mizer/pulp-o-mizer.html. It is basically a pulp magazine cover generator. You don't need to have any graphics skills at all: everything is drag-and-drop, from the font to the background, foreground figures, colours, and so on. These are excellent for promoting science fiction collections, but I also used one to great effect as the opening slide to a presentation that I was giving. You can also use the same service to create desktop wallpapers or website banners.

If you are interested in more traditional posters, there is a wealth of tools available to you. Smore (https://www.smore.com) has a very good reputation. You can design a flyer or poster, share it on social networks and then get analytics on the number of views the poster has had. An alternative comes in the shape of Quozio, at http://quozio.com, which creates attractive quote pictures. You simply enter your quote, attribute it, and then Quozio will provide you with lots of different backgrounds and fonts that you can use to create something that's really attractive and looks good either printed out or shared online.

If you have problems sourcing images to use for promotional posters there are plenty of sites that you can visit which are designed for exactly that purpose. Of course, a lot of them are commercial, and you do have to pay to use the images that you want (usually as a simple small one-off payment), but equally there are plenty of other excellent sources that offer material for free. Since there are so many I won't bother to go into great detail about them, but will merely suggest that you might want to take a look at a few:

- Everystockphoto, www.everystockphoto.com
- FreeImages, www.freeimages.co.uk
- Free Range Stock, http://freerangestock.com
- Kozzi, www.kozzi.com
- Public Domain Photos, www.public-domain-photos.com
- Splashbase, www.splashbase.co
- V like Vintage, www.v-like-vintage.net
- Wikimedia Commons, http://commons.wikimedia.org/wiki/Main_Page
- World images, http://worldimages.sjsu.edu

There are of course many collections available at Flickr, particularly over a million from the British Library (https://www.flickr.com/photos/britishlibrary) the Library of Congress (www.loc.gov/library/libarch-digital.html) and Getty Images (www.gettyimages.co.uk), with its collection of 35 million images.

Another type of image that is very popular is 'word clouds'. These are collections of words (some larger than others, based on the number of times that the specific word is mentioned in the chosen text) produced in the form of a cloud. They can be used to highlight a very wide variety of things. For example, you could take a Shakespeare play and run it through a word cloud creator, save it and then turn it into a poster. You could take the chapter of a book and do the same thing. If you have run an event, take the feedback and put it into a word cloud. If there's something that's particularly in the news, such as a particular politician's speech, or a State of the Union address, its words can easily be captured and put into a word cloud. The cloud can then be printed out, embedded in a blog, put on a Facebook page, placed on a website or shared on Pinterest. As you would expect by now, there are a lot of word cloud packages available. The two most popular ones are Wordle, at www.wordle.net, and Tagxedo, at www.tagxedo.com, which I think is rather more sophisticated, since it allows users to put word clouds into shapes that they choose, rather than the traditional cloud. An example that I created is shown in Figure 9.3, taken from the Wikipedia entry for Sherlock Holmes. In total this took about five minutes to create and required no artistic skill whatsoever.

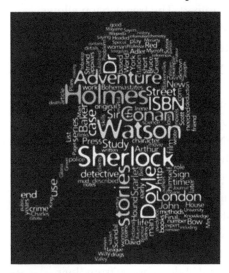

Figure 9.3
A Tagxedo word cloud of Sherlock Holmes

Photographic manipulation

If you're a poor photographer, or you don't have the skills needed to turn fairly run-of-the-mill photographs into miniature works of art, don't despair. There are a lot of really good, entirely free packages that are available directly from the browser and which don't need downloading in order to use. Simply upload the photograph that you want to work with and then choose any of the wide range of filters on offer to alter the image. My personal favourite is Picmonkey, at www.picmonkey.com. It has options for basic edits, such as cropping, rotating, changing the exposure, sharpening or resizing. You can also choose from a range of effects to soften the image, make it black and white or sepia, give the picture dark or frosted edges, or turn it into a drawing. If you have taken photographs of people you can fix blemishes, whiten teeth, apply eye shadow or remove 'red eye'. You can add text, add overlays, put a frame around the image or play with various themes such as zombies, school, sweethearts or Santa Land. There are also a lot of other options, available on subscription. Once you have manipulated your photograph to your satisfaction you can then save it and use it however you see fit. If you are not enamoured of that tool, try Pixlr, at http://pixlr.com, which has a very traditional Photoshop type of interface, Pimagic, at http://app.pikock.com/pimagic or Picfont, at http://picfont.com, to add text to an image.

Make images more exciting

While an image is worth a thousand words, it's even more powerful when you can actually automate it, by adding in more and turning it into a video presentation. Animoto, at http://animoto.com, is designed to create rich videos based on photographs that you upload. The free version allows users to create videos up to 30 seconds in length, while a paid version at £5 a month creates videos up to 10 minutes in length. The process is simple – just upload your photographs (as many as you like), from either your computer or any of a number of social media platforms, choose a style and then Animoto does the rest. You can embed the finished video, share it on Facebook, put it on YouTube or simply link people to it. You can see an example that I made at http://bit.ly/1nNcN0M and it's also on my YouTube channel at http://youtu.be/kgAhj0UNhFw. If Animoto isn't to your taste then try MyPicPals, at http://mypicpals.com, which works on a similar principle except that it doesn't use sound and transition between photographs is slightly more basic. Alternatively, Kizoa (www.kizoa.com) can be used to create videos, slideshows or collages. Once again, it's simplicity itself to use. Simply upload the images that you want to include, choose from any one of dozens of different styles, choose from their licensed music or add your own, add in text, choose your transition styles and then sit back and watch the video being produced. As always, you can then embed, link or share it across social media. An example that I quickly created can be seen again on my YouTube channel at http://youtu.be/cLcVAT_HhKc.

This is a really exciting way of promoting what your library is doing. If you want to simply increase awareness of the library take some photographs of it, include images of the staff (if they're happy with that, of course), throw in some good quotes from users and you've got a really nice video that can go onto the website; you can link to it from social media platforms. Similarly, if you're running an event, take photographs, encourage visitors to the event to do the same and get them to send them to you, and make a memory video of the day. If you have been running a conference you could create a quick montage of key moments and have it running in the background before the last session – this was done at the CILIP Umbrella 2013 Conference and you can see the result at http://youtu.be/dNytmJXvd_s?list=UUNHu-vvcySJJJlIue1VUYQw.

Pinterest

Pinterest (https://uk.pinterest.com) can easily be described as 'bookmarking for images'; when you find an image on the internet that you want to keep you can 'pin' it to your account, rather than having to download it and store it. The service was first conceived in 2009, and it was launched the following year. It's a particularly popular social media destination and it reached 10 million users in a third of the time it took Twitter to do so. It is one of the leading traffic sources in the world, which is to say that people find images that interest them on Pinterest, the image links back to the website or blog, and people then visit to view the page. The majority of users of the service are women (there are various figures to choose from, but they generally show female usage to be around the 80% mark) and popular subjects are food and drink, and fashion and design. Businesses are using Pinterest to promote their products and services visually, with the average order amount placed being US $80 (statistics from www.digitalsherpa.com/blog/25-amazing-pinterest-facts/).

There are various ways that librarians can make use of Pinterest. The first, as consumers, is simply to use it to find good quality images. The people who use the service ('Pinners') generally pin good quality images, often of a much higher quality than those that more traditional search engines display. Of course, it's necessary to go right back to the originating site to check on the Creative Commons status of the image, but it can be a very good starting point. Once a board has been created (you can think of a board as being a folder – it's really only the terminology that's different) you can pin images into it, making it easy to go back and look for specific types of image; librarians in particular often share rights with others so that they can collaborate. An example of such a board is 'The Librarian's List' at www.pinterest.com/ofallonlibrary/the-librarians-list/, which currently has over 4000 pinned images with over 31,000 followers, and over 1000 people who are able to edit the board to add more images. So if your library has specific interests it may be worth investigating whether there is a board that already matches those interests, with a view to becoming a joint author of it.

Librarians can also use Pinterest as creators of content. Create an account and publicize it so that people can start to follow you to see the material that you're pinning. If you have images that you want to share, they can immediately be uploaded into boards that you have created so that other people are able to access them. You can add in your own comments about the images, as can the other participants. People can also 're-pin' images and add them to their own boards, sharing with their own networks of friends and colleagues. You can pin images from your websites and blogs as well. When you create an account, Pinterest gives you the opportunity to add a small bookmarklet to your browser, which you can simply click on when you see an image (yours or someone else's) that you want to pin. This will then activate a small dialogue box enabling you to choose the folder that the image will go into. It's also worth considering adding a 'Pin this' button onto your image web pages, which makes the process that much easier for the visitors to the pages.

Pinterest has recently added an option to allow users to create pins that have a geographic association by adding pins to a map; so, for example, it would be easy to create a literary map of a county by pinning images from the covers of books found on Amazon directly into such a map.

There are a few other ways that librarians can promote the library by using Pinterest .They might showcase their archives of interesting or historical artefacts. A reading club could pin books to create reading lists, and, since Pinterest also allows videos to be added to collections, this could also include book trailers or reviews. If there has been an event in the library and people have taken photographs of it, it might be worth creating a board to share the activities with other people. Members of staff can be introduced by pinning photographs of them into an appropriate Pinterest board. How about highlighting interesting things around the community such as historic buildings, comparing old and new photographs of the same place, or sharing drawings that children have done? And so on. The list of Pinterest uses is limited only by your imagination.

There are obviously copyright issues here; simply because images are available on Pinterest does not mean that they can be used without restriction. If you upload an image the copyright holder – whether you or someone else – still retains all of their rights. I would suggest that, if you find an image on Pinterest that you want to use in some way, you go back to the original source to check the copyright restrictions, and/or contact the owner of the image first.

Flickr

If Pinterest is the new kid on the block, Flickr at www.flickr.com is one of the older inhabitants, founded in 2004. It currently hosts over five billion images (www.statisticbrain.com/social-networking-statistics/) and has gone from being a commercial service to an entirely free one, each user being given enough free space to store up to 500,000 photographs. It's widely used by organizations that want to share large number of photographs – the Library of Congress account at www.flickr.com/photos/library_of_congress/ is sharing over 22,000 photographs.

Anyone can create an account and upload their photographs, images or short video clips and either keep them private or share them with other people. There is, for example, a nice collection of images in the 'Libraries and Librarians' group at www.flickr.com/groups/librariesandlibrarians/ and 4300 members have shared over 50,000 images. If you have images that you wish to share with other people, Flickr is a good tool to use; while it is very similar to Pinterest I think that the search functionality is far superior; it's very easy to tag images with Creative Commons licenses and allow other people to find and then re-use them, which in turn helps to promote your images and collections.

Instagram

There are of course many ways that you can make images available and we've already looked at a few – posting them directly to Pinterest, sharing them on Flickr, or adding them to a Facebook account, for example. However, there are also plenty of applications that work with smartphones and tablets that make the process even easier. In the 'old days' it was necessary to take your photograph, copy it across onto your computer and then upload it to the place you wanted to share it. Nowadays this process is far simpler – simply take a photograph or video on your smartphone, choose a filter to change the look and feel of it if you want, and then post it directly to Facebook or Twitter, for example. Instagram (http://instagram.com) was launched in 2010 and was acquired by Facebook in April 2012, and as of September 2013 it had over 150 million active monthly users. As you would expect with a social media platform people can follow other people, and as of August 2014 the most followed person was Justin Bieber with over 20 million followers.

Instagram can be used by librarians to show off their collections, such as Boston Public Library at http://instagram.com/p/gN3tESHeLi/, or to capture events that have taken place, or perhaps to share their history with archived images. Alternatively (or as well) you might use it in exactly the same way that you can use Pinterest, by sharing pictures of staff, book covers, and so on.

Choices, choices!

At this point you could be forgiven for beginning to wonder which service you should use, and I wouldn't blame you at all. It's of course entirely up to you, but if we look back at activities, rather than the tools, things do become a little easier. If you're an active Facebook user then Instagram is a great tool to be able to quickly and easily share your images on the site, and indeed across onto Twitter as well. The 'here and now', 'this is happening today' news approach works well with Instagram. If you have a large number of items that you'd like to upload to share with people, Flickr may be a better choice, since you will have a great deal of free storage space and an excellent search engine to back it up. On the other hand, if you're particularly interested in promoting your images, and getting other people to help, then Pinterest might be the best avenue to explore.

Infographics

The internet is increasingly become a visual medium, and you can see this in action by exploring the phenomena of infographics. An infographic is simply a visual representation of something – often facts and figures, but it could just as easily be a comparison of two different things, a flow chart, a history of something or just an attractive way of displaying information to make it a little more memorable. In order to get a clearer idea of these things, nip across to your favourite search engine and run a search, popping in the word 'infographic' at the end. You'll be astonished at just how many different images you'll find. Alternatively, use one of the infographic-specific search engines such as Visual.ly at www.visual.ly. Having looked at some, you may well be feeling a little daunted at this stage, because they're often very clever, colourful and well thought out. However, you don't need to be a graphic designer to create a good infographic – lots of sites will provide you with templates or click and drag interfaces. For example, if you wanted to create a CV or resumé, try Vizualize.me at http://vizualize.me/. There are dozens of free templates over at Easel.ly, and Piktochart provides free and commercial themes over at http://piktochart.com/.

Infographics make great marketing and promotional tools; people remember images quickly and easily, while text is far harder. Having infographics in blog posts increases the chance of them being shared by up to 832% (www.mediabistro.com/alltwitter/infographics-on-twitter_b26840).

Bigger images increase readers' engagement with content by up to 600% (www.poynter.org/uncategorized/24963/eyetrack-iii-what-news-websites-look-like-through-readers-eyes/). Of course, there's no reason to simply use infographics online – they can also make fantastic eye-catching posters if you print them out and put them up on the wall!

Podcasting

A podcast is just the fancy name for recording your voice, saving a file, uploading it somewhere and then letting other people listen to it – either directly online or by downloading the file directly onto their mp3 player or iPod (hence the name). This is a really easy way to promote library-based activities: it's simple, effective and can be entirely free. In order to create podcasts you will need a couple of items, both software and hardware. You will use the software to create the recording, to add in any background tracks or music, any effects that you want (such as intro music fading out) and the ability to edit out any coughs or splutters. The software most often used for this purpose is called Audacity, which you can download and use for free from http://audacity.sourceforge.net. You will also need a microphone. You may already have one if you have a laptop with a webcam built in or if you have a webcam that you plug into your desktop, which of course will have a microphone; alternatively, you can simply purchase a headset with a microphone for a few pounds. Obviously the more money you spend, the better the recording will sound, but this does not have to be a large outlay. The technicalities are so simple I can summarize them in a couple of lines. Plug in your microphone, start Audacity, hit the red 'record' button and say what you want to say. Then stop recording and save what you've done. It really is almost that simple, but as with most things, if you want to do it well, you need to give it some thought.

You have to get the basics right. What do you want to say? There's no point sitting there and chattering aimlessly, because no one is going to want to listen to that! Have a clear plan of what you intend talking about and make some notes. Improvising will not work but, equally, reading from a prepared script makes you sound dull and lifeless. Choose an optimum length for the podcast: if it's too long people won't listen to the entire thing, and if it's too short they'll probably pass it by. Initially aim for perhaps 20 minutes in length, building up over time as you become more comfortable. You'll have to record some audio and then play it back and make sure that it sounds good. Don't try and record in a busy library environment because that will in all probability sound pretty dire. You'll learn by trial and error how close to get to the microphone and how loudly you have to speak. Be yourself and sound enthusiastic; people enjoy enthusiasm and it makes the podcast a real pleasure to listen to. Decide if you are going to be the main or only presenter, or get other colleagues involved so that they can take over and talk about different subjects, and perhaps have guest podcasters whom you can interview. Don't worry too much about 'fluffing your lines', since you can always go back and edit out the mistake; what I generally do is continue recording, swear for a bit and then leave a nice long gap of about 5 seconds' silence. You'll find that easy to see when you go back and edit out the error (and the swearing!) and no one will know the difference.

Once you have recorded the podcast you'll want to have somewhere that you can host it. There are plenty of sites that will happily put your podcast online for free, though they will in all probability limit the amount that you can store on their servers and the amount of bandwidth you can use per month. Podbean, at www.podbean.com, offers a complete package, allowing you to upload, manage and promote your podcasts with the minimum of fuss. Spreaker, at www.spreaker.com, will also host for you, and you can also broadcast live if you wish to. Podomatic, at https://www.podomatic.com, has an excellent collection of podcasts if you just want to listen to a few in order to get your bearings, and of course you can add your own. Most of these tend to focus on their commercial offerings (which to be fair are not that expensive), but if you are really tight on a budget, you could try Audioboo, at http://audioboo.fm, which also allows you to record directly on the site, will offer you three minutes' worth of audio – not enough for a long podcast, it's true, but you have no limit on the number you can upload, and regularly used accounts tend to get more attention. Soundcloud (https://soundcloud.com) has an emphasis on music, but you can also just record a traditional voice-only podcast which they can host for you. Alternatively, you can get the Internet Archive to host your podcast for you, entirely free of charge, though you do have to register with them first, at http://archive.org/create.

You may decide that you want to give your podcasts a little bit of polish, by adding in some music or even sound effects. Luckily, there are plenty of search tools that can find free material for you to use. YouTube has added an audio library of free music and sound effects, at https://www.youtube.com/audiolibrary/music. Soundbible (http://soundbible.com) provides free sound clips, sound bites and sound effects, while ccMixter (http://ccmixter.org) is an international community of 40,000 musicians who make their material available under Creative Commons licensing.

Having got the practicalities sorted, you do need to decide what sort of podcast will work best for the users of your library. I would suggest running a quick search for 'library podcasts' because there are thousands of them available. The Seattle Public Library, at www.spl.org/library-collection/podcasts, has a series of author readings and library event podcasts, where authors talk about their own books and give author readings, while local chefs and farmers share stories about growing, cooking and sharing food. The Library of Congress, at www.loc.gov/podcasts, have a series of podcasts designed to allow listeners to discover the treasures of the Library, as seen through the eyes of experts and special guests. The British Library has also produced podcasts covering talks, discussions, interviews and podcasts from science events, offering a list of them at www.bl.uk/whatson/podcasts. Podcasts do not have to be limited to public libraries though – very far from it. There are a wide variety of other types of library that support podcasts – law libraries, podcasts from libraries in the corporate sector, government libraries, school libraries; in fact pretty much any kind of library that you can think of!

If you're still struggling for some ideas, here's a list to keep you going:

- news and events about the library service, and interviews with staff or library users
- news items about the subject area that your information service covers
- frequently asked questions
- a guided audio tour of the library
- 'how-to' articles on a wide variety of subjects, such as internet search, obtaining a book via interlibrary loan, database searching
- items about the company you work for, or the community that your library supports
- two-person discussions about subjects of interest
- do an 'outside broadcast' – if you're attending a conference or exhibition, take along a digital voice recorder and do some narration or vox pop interviews
- record a book club discussion and turn it into a podcast
- create a podcast around a blog post that you've written – ask your patrons what they would like to listen to.

When you have created the podcast you can put it online with one of the hosting services that I've mentioned, and embed it in your website or blog. Then you can share it across social media; link to it from Twitter, Facebook and LinkedIn. Add a really attractive picture to the web page that you've embedded it on and then pin that image into Pinterest. Don't forget – if you produce something on social media, share it far and wide.

Video

There's no doubt that a video is one of the quickest ways to promote and market. People love watching and sharing videos and sometimes they go viral, meaning they get shared, viewed, re-shared and so on into the hundreds of thousands or even millions of views. The most viewed YouTube video of all time (as of July 2014) is 'Gangnam Style' by Psy, with 2,043,738,264 views. In the area of librarianship the most famous video is probably The Dewey Decimal Rap, with 1,513,482 hits, with 'Librarians Do Gaga' with 926,497 videos coming in second. There are lots of theories as to what makes a video go viral, but my own feeling is that it's really down to dumb luck, being in the right place at the right time and hitching a ride on a existing meme (an idea, behaviour or style that spreads from person to person within a culture). While these are fun to watch most of us have to have a rather more realistic view of what we're able to do.

Creating videos doesn't have to be difficult; in fact as we've already seen, it's possible to put some still images together and turn them into a very basic video. If you have access to a smartphone you could always explore the idea of a Vine video. Vine (https://vine.co) is really the Twitter of video, with each one being only six seconds long. You may wonder what can be achieved in six seconds, but then people said the same thing about 140 characters not so long ago! In truth, a Vine video doesn't have to be six sequential seconds of video; you can record a second, pause, record another second and so on, so it's quite good for very short stop-film animation. Vine provides librarians with lots of different ways to market and promote their services:

- introduce yourself and your colleagues with a quick wave and a smile
- do the same thing with any new books or other resources that you have recently obtained
- quick guided tours of the library and library exhibits

- behind-the-scenes tours of a library or setting up for an exhibition
- library montages
- basic instructional videos and tips
- quick (very quick!) answers to frequently asked questions
- a vox pop of a conference or exhibition
- six-second book reviews.

Some early adopters of Vine are:

- UCLA Powell Library (https://vine.co/v/brBgBDKIIet)
- the Topeka and Shawnee County Public Library
  (https://vine.co/topekalibrary)
- Brookline Library (https://vine.co/u/911702113355186176)
- Plymouth Libraries (https://vine.co/u/910170463639052288)
- New York Institute of Technology (https://vine.co/u/907714337093861376)
- Lansdowne Library (https://vine.co/u/907764744784592896).

Of course, Vine isn't going to send visitors flocking to your library or your website, but it will help with the drip effect; as advised with podcasting, share your Vine videos far and wide.

Unfortunately there isn't space or time in this book to go into great detail about the practicalities of creating videos, and there are plenty of other titles that specialize in this area. Very briefly, however: you can create video with an increasing array of tools, from a smartphone to a tablet (and if you're using Apple products the iMovie app is an excellent product to edit with) to a full-blown digital recorder of some type. If you're short on budget you might want to explore Windows Movie Maker, which does a good job, and isn't hard to learn. Once you have created a video there are plenty of tools that you can use to adapt and use it. Magisto, at www.magisto.com, for example, allows users to upload video and still images and it is able to blend both together. It includes excellent transitions and music and turns the video on and off, including slow motion. You can also share it across platforms as you would expect. If you're interested in taking a look (and if you like dogs!) you can take a look at one that I created, at www.magisto.com/video/M0EcYFIMCCg0AxZnCzE. Alternatively, take a look at Blendspace, at https://www.blendspace.com, which allows you to combine videos and images together to create collaborative research presentations, digital storytelling and training sessions.

If you already have uploaded videos to YouTube you can actually edit them using software provided by Google, which you can locate at https://www.youtube.com/editor. You can edit out material, change the orientation (excellent if you have taken a video with an iPhone in portrait mode), add titles and music, combine two or more videos, add slow motion, blur faces, add filters, include annotations and add subtitles. It's a powerful and easy-to-use tool, with the added advantage that it's entirely free to use. The Mozilla Popcorn Maker, at https://popcorn.webmaker.org, has similar functionality, but the major difference is that you can work on anyone's video, not just your own. A slight twist on editing your own video is provided by The Madvideo resource (www.themadvideo.com). This allows you to add in tags to a video which viewers can then roll over with their mouse to stop the video automatically and enlarge the tag to provide links and content. You could therefore easily create a 'how-to' video of ways to search the library catalogue and have tags popping up at different points, allowing people to visit the catalogue immediately, run a task, then come back and continue watching the video. Finally, embedplus, at www.embedplus.com, is a powerful set of tools that enhance YouTube videos simply and easily.

Of course, this does presuppose that you will have a YouTube channel already, but if you haven't it's easy enough to get, and in fact if you already have a Google account you have a YouTube channel. I would recommend uploading any videos that you create onto YouTube; it makes it very easy to embed them on your own platforms, or share them directly across social media resources. You will also get a set of analytical tools to keep track of how many views each has had. Some people tell me that they're slightly worried about using free video tools, especially if the tool disappears, but if you have a copy of the video and you've put it onto YouTube, it's there for however long you want it, even if the original tool used to create it disappears.

Augmented reality

Augmented reality is defined by Wikipedia as:

> a live direct or indirect view of a physical, real-world environment whose elements are augmented (or supplemented) by computer-generated sensory input such as sound, video, graphics or GPS data. It is related to a more general concept called mediated reality, in which a view of reality is modified (possibly

even diminished rather than augmented) by a computer. As a result, the technology functions by enhancing one's current perception of reality.

http://en.wikipedia.org/wiki/Augmented_reality

Put into English that essentially means that if you use the camera on your smartphone or tablet in conjunction with a piece of software you'll see stuff that isn't there. For example, when I park my car I can use an app called CarFinder, which checks the GPS coordinates of my car. I can then go off and shop, and when I need to get back to the car, I turn on the app, look through the camera display on my smartphone and follow the red arrow that I can see superimposed on the road in front of me until I get back to where I started.

Now, at first glance this doesn't seem too helpful when it comes to a library environment, but there are numerous ways in which it can be. For example, one app called Aurasma (www.aurasma.com) allows you to create effects very simply and easily. You start with a 'trigger' image; it may be a logo, photograph, 'real' item such as a dollar bill, and then you choose an action that takes place when someone views it using the app on their smartphone or tablet. So, for example, it would be simplicity itself to have a book cover as a trigger image, and when viewed using the app a video plays with a member of staff reviewing the title. Alternatively, the same concept could be used as a training aid – have a trigger image next to a computer and viewers could then get a short tutorial on how to search for information, or the best way to use a library catalogue. How about a series of trigger images that could be used for induction and guiding people around a collection? In case you're wondering how this works for marketing or promotion, as long as someone has the Aurasma app (which is free) and they have subscribed to your channel, they could access library promotional material from anywhere. Links could take people to YouTube videos, web pages or even Twitter accounts. Augmented reality can be used to surround ancient manuscripts with digital content, allowing students and researchers to access supporting material quickly and easily. The Scarlet Project at MIMAS is a good example of this and you can read more about it at http://teamscarlet.wordpress.com/showcase.

Summary

As you can see, there are plenty of ways in which you can promote and market your services, and I have just concentrated on a few that really work around multimedia-based tools. I would recommend trying out a lot of different approaches; you never know what will work best for you until you have had a chance to play with them. Don't forget, though, that one of the most important things you can do when you put this information out into the public domain is to share it as far and as wide as possible, not just once but several times. Once you have created something that also gives you an opportunity to blog about what you did and the lessons that you learned, which can then be tweeted and added to Facebook, and so on.

URLs mentioned in this chapter

Animoto http://animoto.com
- Author's example animation http://bit.ly/1nNcN0M, http://youtu.be/kgAhj0UNhFw

Audacity http://audacity.sourceforge.net

Audioboo http://audioboo.fm

Aurasma www.aurasma.com

BigHugeLabs http://bighugelabs.com

Blendspace https://www.blendspace.com

British Library podcasts www.bl.uk/whatson/podcasts

ccMixter http://ccmixter.org

embedplus www.embedplus.com

Everystockphoto www.everystockphoto.com

Flickr www.flickr.com
- British Library images https://www.flickr.com/photos/britishlibrary
- Libraries and Librarians www.flickr.com/groups/librariesandlibrarians/
- Library of Congress www.flickr.com/photos/library_of_congress/

Free Range Stock http://freerangestock.com

FreeImages www.freeimages.co.uk

Getty Images www.gettyimages.co.uk

Instagram http://instagram.com
- Boston Public Library http://instagram.com/p/gN3tESHeLi/

Internet Archive http://archive.org/create

Keepcalm-o-matic www.keepcalm-o-matic.co.uk

Kizoa www.kizoa.com

- Author's example animations:
  http://youtu.be/cLcVAT_HhKc,
  http://youtu.be/dNytmJXvd_s?list=UUNHu-vvcySJJJllue1VUYQw

Kozzi www.kozzi.com

Library of Congress podcasts www.loc.gov/podcasts

Madvideo www.themadvideo.com

Magisto www.magisto.com
- Author's example site
  www.magisto.com/video/M0EcYFlMCCg0AxZnCzE

Mozilla PopcornMaker https://popcorn.webmaker.org

MyPicPals http://mypicpals.com

Picfont http://picfont.com

Picmonkey www.picmonkey.com

Piktochart http://piktochart.com/

Pimagic http://app.pikock.com/pimagic

Pinterest https://uk.pinterest.com
- The Librarian's List
  www.pinterest.com/ofallonlibrary/the-librarians-list/

Pixlr http://pixlr.com

Podbean www.podbean.com

Podomatic https://www.podomatic.com

Public Domain Photos www.public-domain-photos.com

Pulp-o-mizer http://thrilling-tales.webomator.com/derange-o-lab/
  pulp-o-mizer/pulp-o-mizer.html

Quozio http://quozio.com

Scarlet Project at MIMAS http://teamscarlet.wordpress.com/showcase

Seattle Public Library podcasts www.spl.org/library-collection/podcasts

Smore https://www.smore.com

Soundbible http://soundbible.com

Soundcloud https://soundcloud.com

Splashbase www.splashbase.co

Spreaker www.spreaker.com

Tagxedo www.tagxedo.com

V like Vintage www.v-like-vintage.net

Vine https://vine.co
- Examples of Vine videos:
  UCLA Powell Library https://vine.co/v/brBgBDKllet, the Topeka
  and Shawnee County Public Library https://vine.co/topekalibrary,

Brookline Library https://vine.co/u/911702113355186176,
Plymouth Libraries https://vine.co/u/910170463639052288,
New York Institute of Technology
https://vine.co/u/907714337093861376, Lansdowne Library
https://vine.co/u/907764744784592896

Visual.ly www.visual.ly

Vizualize.me http://vizualize.me/

Wikimedia Commons http://commons.wikimedia.org/wiki/Main_Page

Wordle www.wordle.net

World images http://worldimages.sjsu.edu

YouTube audio library https://www.youtube.com/audiolibrary/music

YouTube video editor https://www.youtube.com/editor

Visit the Facet Publishing YouTube channel
(www.youtube.com/user/facetpublishing) for Phil Bradley's video
A guide to creating promotional material for free using Big Huge
Labs – and more.

CHAPTER 10

Creating a social media policy

Introduction

A question that I often ask delegates on courses is: 'Does your organization have a social media policy?' and the answer is usually in the negative. I have long ceased to be surprised by this since it's the norm rather than the exception. Indeed, in a recent FT-ICSA Boardroom Bellwether report (https://www.icsa.org.uk/assets/files/pdfs/Business%20Bellwether/icsa-ft-bellwether-5.pdf) 47% of respondents said that their board had never discussed a social media policy and 39% had only discussed it between one and three times. Only 7% said that their board had discussed social media more often. Furthermore, only 26% of respondents stated that a social media strategy was important, with 65% describing it as neutral or unimportant. I think that there are many reasons for this, some of which I have previously mentioned; they are unfamiliar with social media either in practice or concept, and they find the terminology of likes, followers, tweets and so on something they dislike or feel uncomfortable about. The end result is that employees, who are often far more familiar with social media, don't feel that they are being given support; they're unsure on what they are allowed to do and what they shouldn't do, leading to a situation where they do nothing, or go off in a whole host of different directions with little help or guidance.

A good social media policy will protect the staff and the library; it will mean that they are able to work on social media with much more confidence, difficult situations can be handled swiftly and effectively, and the entire organization will benefit rather than suffer. In this chapter I'll look at some of the things that you can take into account when putting a policy together, and as a humorous aside we can take a look at some organizations who didn't think that far ahead and what happened as a result.

Why an organization needs a social media policy

A statement on why an organization needs and wants to have a social media policy should be right at the heart and the start of any document. It will help set the structure and give employees a clear idea of what is expected of them by the organization, how they are to implement it, and for what purpose. Part of the guidelines for BT say:

> BT recognises that its transformation into a global communication services company delivering software driven products relies on a workforce that can actively participate in collaboration and innovation with colleagues, customers, partners and suppliers on the web using social media tools.
>
> It is therefore important that we all understand how social media tools can help BT achieve its business objectives and that we are empowered to contribute effectively to this collaborative activity on the web when it supports our roles within the organisation.

They then go on to point out that:

> Any BT person can use social media tools on the BT Intranet without approval. BT people may also use social media tools on the internet in support of their role and where there is clear business benefit provided they have permission to do so from their line manager.
>
> http://richarddennison.wordpress.com/bts-social-media-guidelines

It's therefore clear to everyone in the organization exactly why BT wants to get involved with social media – to achieve their aims and activities, and there's clear encouragement to let as many people as possible get involved with using different tools in support of their role and activities.

The Greteman Group have a similar understanding:

> At Greteman Group, we not only embrace the media and technology that make these bombardments possible, we harness them for our clients. We also welcome the power of individuals to leverage and enhance their personal brands through these tools.
>
> www.gretemangroup.com/social-media-policy

I think that the use of the phrase 'personal brands' here is quite important, since they understand that it's in the interests of the company to encourage employees to get involved with social media both for the benefit of the company, but also as individuals.

The National Library of Australia follows a similar pattern:

> The Library encourages all employees to communicate online in many ways, such as through social media, professional networking sites, blogs, online news sites and personal web sites. However, all employees need to use good judgment about what material appears online, and in what context.
>
> https://www.nla.gov.au/policy-and-planning/social-media

What all of these policies have in common, of course, is an open approach to using social media-based tools and a realization that it's in their best interests to do so.

Defining social media

Hopefully one of the things that has become clear throughout the course of this book is that 'social media' is not exactly a strict term with clear definitions. Consequently any social media policy needs to have some indication as to exactly what is being referred to. I have seen policies that make a distinction between different tools such as Twitter and Facebook, but, as you'll also know by now, I prefer to consider activities, rather than tools, so this doesn't particularly work for me. It makes little sense to break down the subject, so a general definition that doesn't tie anyone down is more helpful. The Chartered Institute of Public Relations has a good definition:

> Social media is the term commonly given to Internet and mobile-based channels and tools that allow users to interact with each other and share opinions and content. As the name implies, social media involves the building of communities or networks and encouraging participation and engagement.
>
> www.cipr.co.uk/content/social-media-guidance

This is a nicely open-ended definition with the right balance of tools and activities mentioned in the mix.

Social media policies for specific tools

As I have just mentioned, the idea of specific policies for specific tools doesn't particularly appeal to me, but I'm not writing this book for my benefit, and I know that some people do want guidelines for particular tools, so in this section I'll attempt to point out some things to take into account.

Twitter

If your library is going to have a Twitter account it will be necessary to decide on the name of the account, if it's to be a generic account, or the names of individuals who can indicate who they work for in the account name. The biography needs to be correctly filled out, with a link to the library home page, or preferably to a page on the website that goes into detail about what people can expect from the account. The Twitter account of the Department of Work and Pensions page lists all the different accounts that they run, which specific team runs each account, when it's managed (that is to say, normal office hours) and what followers can expect to see by way of tweets. They also point out that following an account does not imply any kind of endorsement; particularly important if your library account follows authors, publishers and the like.

One slightly contentious point regarding Twitter in particular (but all social media platforms in general) is the use of levity. Some policies are very strict in this area; Walmart for example state:

> Walmart wants to make sure its employees who are 'official' Twitter users for Walmart are identified as such, stick to customer replies, and focus on this alone. Walmart's Twitter users should only talk about Walmart and not engage in unnecessary banter.
>
> http://corporate.walmart.com/social-media-guidelines

There is, of course, a real need to be serious and professional in dealing with clients and customers, but this might be seen as being overly stern. If the activity behind a Twitter account is to correspond and interact with people, then the occasional joke or 'have a nice weekend' tweet may well assist rather than detract from that goal.

A policy relating to Twitter should make some mention of hashtags; which ones are appropriate to use (possibly with a list of organizational ones), when to use them, how many to use, and which ones shouldn't be used. There should also be mention of the fact that staff shouldn't simply jump onto a trending hashtag and start using it; that's generally regarded as hashtag spam and is frowned upon.

One-to-one tweeting and direct messaging are also subjects that should be covered. Is it acceptable to send out a private tweet in answer to a public question? If so, is there a limit on the type of information that is going to be included?

Staff need to clearly understand the legal responsibilities of their involvement in Twitter. All too many people still seem to think that Twitter is some sort of 'Wild West' with no laws governing their behaviour, but this is very far from the truth. There have been several occasions when people have received prison sentences for things that they have posted. It's generally best not to actively participate in general news stories (particularly political ones) unless that's central to the organization's activities, but even then, a neutral stance should be taken; if in doubt, check the intended tweet with a line manager – alternatively, if you think you need to check it, you probably shouldn't be thinking of sending it in the first place!

Facebook

A Facebook policy should outline what the intended purpose of the account is, such as to provide information and updates regarding the library, its personnel, activities and events. Staff who post to a Facebook account need to be named, and clearly indicate that they are employees: not necessarily in every post, of course, since that would quickly get tedious, but there really should be no doubt if the person posting is a member of staff or not. Staff should be clear on what is appropriate to post, and that posts should be respectful and considerate, and not to contain vulgarity, threats or abusive language.

Since other people can post to a Facebook page it's necessary to have an indication (preferably through a link to a social media policy statement on the website) as to what is acceptable, and what is not. It's sensible to retain the right to remove certain types of posting, such as obscene or racist content, libellous statements, plagiarized material, commercial promotions, and so on.

As with Twitter, it may be worth making a statement to the effect that 'liking' other pages should not be construed as any kind of endorsement. Since Facebook relies on advertising on its pages it may also be worth making the point that the library or organization disassociates itself from any and all advertising that readers may see, and that the existence of any such adverts do not relate in any way to the organization itself.

Blogs

As you would expect by now, a blogging policy should be clear on the purpose of the blog, and the activities that it supports. A blog (or indeed any number of blogs if the organization or library is that enlightened!) may well be written by a number of different people, so it's necessary to define the 'voice' of the blog; is it entirely serious, factual and without frivolity, or is a level of 'playfulness' acceptable? How long should blog posts be: short and to the point, or can they be much longer, and involve an element of personal or professional observation and comment?

Some blogs do not allow comments, and there may well be good reasons for this, but it should be the exception, rather than the rule. Of course, there's no reason why one blog post should not allow comments, while the rest of them do; there doesn't need to be a hard-and-fast rule, but staff should know when and why to implement it. Most blog comments are moderated (i.e. checked by a member of staff) – given the amount of spam that any post will generate it's the only sensible approach to take. However, comments should be made public as soon as is practical and blog commentators need to know what is acceptable and what is not.

If anything is factually incorrect in a blog posting it should be corrected as quickly as possible, fairly obviously. However, rather than simply delete the factual inaccuracy it might be preferable to add an edit to clarify and put right the error. While it's very easy to simply delete and replace, people do not tend to take kindly to that (in the same way that they dislike it when tweets are deleted) and there's always the danger that someone may have taken a screenshot of the inaccuracy, and rather than solve the problem, it's just been compounded.

Personal versus professional

Let's get this one out of the way quickly, because it's an easy one to deal with. All of the social media policies that I have looked at will almost without exception make a distinction between what people do in their own time and what they do in work time. The BBC guidelines are particularly helpful here:

> Your own personal activity, done for your friends and contacts, but not under or in the name of BBC News. You are not discouraged from doing any of this, but as a BBC member of staff – and especially as someone who works in News – there are particular considerations to bear in mind. They can all be summarised as: 'Don't do anything stupid'.
>
> http://news.bbc.co.uk/1/shared/bsp/hi/pdfs/ 14_07_11_news_social_media_guidance.pdf

They go on to make the point that even if people are acting in their own personal capacity they are on show to their friends, so don't say anything in an openly partisan way, don't bring the BBC into disrepute, don't criticize colleagues or sanitize Wikipedia pages. They also make the important point that staff should not use their name or title to include BBC in any form at all.

This makes perfect sense – it's perhaps slightly stricter than you'll find with other policies, but that's due to the particular nature of the BBC, and the high level of visibility of their staff. It's also worth staff including a statement somewhere in their personal details along the lines of 'The views expressed here are my own and do not necessarily reflect/represent those of my employer'.

If someone is posting on behalf of their library or organization it may be worth creating accounts that reflect this, referring either to the library name in general, or to a title, rather than a person's name. The reason for this is that if that person then leaves the employment of the company or organization they can't take that account 'with them' as it were, and it allows someone else to come in and take it over, providing consistency.

A separate section of a policy should cover what staff can and cannot do when posting on behalf of the library. South Holland Library has some useful guidance at this point:

- Verify that comments are factual, accurate and presented with correct spelling and grammar.
- Do not post materials that are abusive, obscene, defamatory, threatening, harassing, slanderous, maliciously false, offensive, libellous to the Library, embarrassing or that are discriminatory.

- Realize that Social media communities have their own culture, etiquette, and norms and be respectful of them.

www.southhollandlibrary.org/policies/8.0-SocialMediaPolicy.pdf

There's a slight contradiction there between points 1 and 3, since it's regarded as perfectly normal to contract words when writing a tweet, for example, but other than that it covers a lot of the bases that need to be covered, while still leaving staff freedom to communicate and converse with other people.

Some policies do state that their employees' use of social media will be monitored and that certain types of material or posting will not be acceptable. The Haverhill Public Library has a fairly comprehensive collection of what employees should not post:

- Obscene, sexist or racist content
- Personal attacks, insults, or threatening language
- Potentially libelous and slanderous statements
- Plagiarized or copyrighted material
- Private, personal information published without consent
- Comments totally unrelated to the content of the forum
- Hyperlinks to material that is not directly related to the discussion
- Commercial promotions or spam
- Organized political activity
- Photos or other images/media that fall in any of the above categories.

www.haverhillpl.org/about/policies/social-networking-policy

Nothing there is particularly contentious of course, and is entirely common sense, but it does make sense to put it down in writing, not specifically for what employees cannot write about, but more importantly for what they can.

The chain of command

Of course, it's all well and good (and in my view desirable) for as many staff as possible to have access to and to use social media, but that doesn't mean that everyone who sees a tweet or Facebook posting should leap straight on and respond. That might look like overkill, or if you have people contradicting the original poster it might seem like bullying. Equally, however, 72% of people who complain on Twitter expect a response within an hour and 43% expect a brand to respond within an hour on positive feedback (http://blog.hubspot. com/marketing/twitter-response-time-data). If responses aren't forthcoming within this time period 60% of people will take further negative action, such as telling their friends and family about their poor experience or shaming the company in social media, and would not recommend the organization to other people. However, it's not all bad news, because if a brand or company responds in a timely manner 47% would recommend the brand in social media, 43% would encourage their friends and family to buy from that brand, and 42% would praise the company in social media. Now of course, you could argue that a library or information service is not in and of itself a 'brand' and I would agree. However, I don't think it's inaccurate to make the broad point that a lack of quick response leads to disappointment and negative consequences, while a positive and fast response has the opposite effect.

Going back to the BBC News policy, they are very keen that whatever is published on social media 'must have a second pair of eyes prior to publication.' This makes sense, but equally it does slow down the response time. Rather than having someone else check everything that goes out, slowing down the response time and perhaps losing some fun and spontaneity, it may make more sense to say that certain types of communication can be created by specific employees, so for example a tweet promoting a particular event does not need to be double-checked, but a rebuttal to a critical comment on Facebook may require the intervention of someone more senior.

Coca Cola encourage staff to ask as scouts for compliments and criticisms. Their policy states:

> Even if you are not an official online spokesperson for the Company, you are one of our most vital assets for monitoring the social media landscape. If you come across positive or negative remarks about the Company or its brands online that you believe are important, consider sharing them by forwarding them to . . .
>
> www.viralblog.com/wp-content/uploads/2010/01/
> TCCC-Online-Social-Media-Principles-12-2009.pdf

This really encourages everyone to take part in a positive way and gives them a clear chain of command and what to do when something happens. This is also particularly pertinent for information and library staff, who will in all likelihood be spending a lot of each day online looking for and at content, including references to the organization that they work for. They need to know exactly what type of material they need to pass onto a line manager, and the importance of doing so in a speedy manner.

Dealing with criticism

One of the most irritating reasons for not getting involved in social media communications that I hear all the time is 'What if someone says something nasty about us?' This is a question that made sense in the old days, because although people have always made critical comments, they would either address them directly to the organization in question, or by word of mouth to friends and family. So a management structure is often able to see the danger of using social media, in that a critical comment can be widely reported and copied on, but then are often incapable of realizing that they can't stop this happening – their knee-jerk reaction is that if the company isn't using social media then the problem doesn't exist. That's just like a small child covering its eyes and presuming that their parents won't be able to see them. Of course, if a company doesn't work on social media platforms they have little chance of affecting the discussion that surrounds them. At least if someone comes to their Facebook page or their Twitter account they can act quickly and decisively to sort out the problem quickly. In actual fact, reactions to criticism can almost always be used to good effect. If the criticism is valid the response needs to be apologetic, but also constructive, with an indication of what the library or organization is going to do differently in the future. This is obviously hard to do in a 140-character tweet, so it may be best to use a tweet to link to a longer statement on a blog or on the website. If the criticism is invalid then the response can point out how the original poster was incorrect, and making clear exactly what the true situation is. In either case the response should be respectful, clear, authoritative and speedy. Under no circumstances should employees be encouraged to delete a comment on a blog, or on a Facebook page! Deleting critical comments is one of the very worst things that anyone can do, simply it doesn't brush the problem under the carpet, it merely gives the original poster something else to comment on, leading to other people weighing into the discussion as well.

Do's and don'ts

Several policies that I looked at have a long 'do's and don'ts' section, and it was really quite tedious reading through them. The trouble with a list of what you can't do rather implies that everything else you can do, or vice versa, and there's never going to be room to create a document that covers every eventuality. This problem is then compounded when library staff start to use other tools; an entirely new list needs to be written for them, and it's a never-ending task. Of course, a fairly generic list can be created, but much of it is going to be common sense, or covered by other aspects of an employee's contract. It also tends to imply that employees are not sensible enough to work out what is appropriate in a given situation, which is not going to increase staff morale, so I prefer the BBC statement, previously mentioned which states 'Don't do anything stupid'. It's concise, appropriate and treats employees like adults.

Legal issues

I should emphasize at this point that I am not a lawyer, so this section should not be considered as legal advice and any concerns about legality of use with regards social media should be addressed to an appropriately qualified individual.

There are several concerns that staff should all be aware of when it comes to legislation and social media. I'm sure that we're all now aware that people can say the most stupid things on Twitter or Facebook, and they end up in court (or even prison) as a result. Staff should be aware of intellectual property rights, and should therefore only use Creative Commons licensed material, or have the copyright holder's permission to use their content on social media. Staff should have a clear understanding of exactly what copyright means and appreciate the differences between 'rights managed' and 'royalty free' content.

The law also requires that a duty of confidentiality is established, so doctors should not blog about named patients, information staff should not mention new clients before the details are all agreed, and material should not be made available when it is not in the public domain. Then there are defamation laws, and an organization may well be held responsible for something an employee says on a social media account, so it may be worth elaborating on this in a social media policy.

There will almost certainly be specific laws that apply in the country that you happen to be in, so in the United Kingdom we have the Data Protection Act 2008 and we are also subject to the Human Rights Act, which may not apply elsewhere. In the USA there are also the rights guaranteed under the

First Amendment, for example.

It should also be stressed that once information is in the public domain, it cannot be taken back. Tweets get archived instantaneously, Facebook postings can be captured and images on Pinterest can be downloaded. As such, extra care really does have to be taken when creating content that's going to go onto a social media platform.

How often should a policy be reviewed?

I have seen some policies that date back to 2010 or 2011 and while it's impressive that they actually produced something very early on, they are already out of date, since they don't mention a variety of the newer tools such as Pinterest. I think that policies should be under constant review, particularly if they refer to specific tools; a more general policy that refers to social media activities rather less so, perhaps annually.

Summary

When looking for social media policies I found it very difficult to find many that were publicly available from libraries. This may well be because the policy that the library staff use is part and parcel of a rather larger organizational policy, or policies are kept private (which isn't very helpful for library users), or they simply don't exist. There are plenty of general templates that are available which can simply be downloaded and used, but having looked at them, they are generally so broad and general as to be of virtually no use whatsoever. Ideally it's worth looking at a variety of examples and cherry-picking the sections that seem most appropriate. There is a very useful collection of policies at Social Media Governance (http://socialmediagovernance.com/policies) collected from a wide variety of organizations and it's a mine of useful (and not-so-useful) examples.

URLs mentioned in this chapter
Social Media Governance http://socialmediagovernance.com/policies

Visit the Facet Publishing YouTube channel (www.youtube.com/user/facetpublishing) for Phil Bradley's video What is a good social media policy and why is it needed in libraries?

Social media disasters

While it's always useful to look at good examples of social media use and policies, it can actually be more enlightening to look at examples of where the use (or lack of use) of social media has gone disastrously wrong. This final section isn't intended to frighten you or discourage you from using social media – quite the contrary. Good examples of bad use make it much less likely that you'll make the same mistakes and suffer the same ignominies and will in fact be useful supporting evidence to encourage the 'powers that be' not only to use social media platforms, but to use them wisely, supplemented with a good and robust social media policy. There are many examples that I can choose from (although none from the world of library and information science), and I'm sure that you can find plenty of others, but these are just a few of my own favourites.

United Breaks Guitars

This is the title of a song written by a Canadian musician, Dave Carroll, which details his trials and tribulations following the damage to his guitar from poor handling by United Airlines staff. He complained to United Airlines, but unfortunately for them they took no notice of him for nine months, and finally he wrote a protest song that went onto YouTube, *United Breaks Guitars* (https://www.youtube.com/watch?v=5YGc4zOqozo), followed by two more. The first video gained 150,000 views within the day it was released (6 July 2009) and to date has had over 14 million views. The company's belated apologies and offers of compensation were derided and within four days United Airlines' stock price fell by 10%, costing their shareholders about US$180 million in value. Dave Carroll went on to write a book about his experiences and is now in demand as a speaker on customer service.

Perhaps the biggest error that the airline made was not to take the complaint seriously, and to hope that it would just go away. The second error that they made was to underestimate the power of social media, which to be fair to them, was still little-known in 2009. However, if they had treated their customer with respect and attempted to sort out the problem quickly and efficiently the song would never have been written in the first place. The lesson here is that the power of social media is indeed immense and cannot be underestimated. Even a single person can make a huge difference, and the days of control are long gone. Politeness, respect and swift positive responses need to be at the heart of employees' dealings on social media.

Never seconds

On 30 April 2012 a young Scottish schoolgirl, Martha Payne, launched her own blog called 'Never seconds' at http://neverseconds.blogspot.co.uk, in which she documented by word and photograph her school meals. It became of national interest after the school meals campaigner Jamie Oliver saw it and by 15 June it had over 3 million hits. The following day Martha was told by her head teacher that she wasn't allowed to take photographs of her dinner any longer; the decision coming from Argyll and Bute Council, which was concerned about the potential for negative press reaction. This lead to an outcry and following involvement by politicians the council reversed its decision. It was described by one Twitter user as 'A classic example of local government failing to grasp the power of social media @argyllandbute could have made PR gold from #neverseconds.' As of February 2014 the blog has had 10 million hits, it was named as the Observer Food Blog of the Year and had raised over £142,000 for charity. The Council meanwhile had to deal with far more negative press than they were expecting.

This is another example of an organization failing to realize the power of social media, and not taking people seriously – even if the person in question was a schoolgirl. If they had encouraged the blog, provided information about the background to the school dinners on offer, invited Martha to see how meals were created or got her and other pupils involved with the selection of meals they could, as the Twitter user indicated, have given a far better insight into the subject and would have been seen in a far more positive light. Once something is out there in social media it's not going to go away and needs to be dealt with carefully; attempting to ban or control simply will not work.

Tweeting from the wrong handle

In 2011 an employee who was working for Chrysler's social media agency tweeted to the @ChryslerAutos account 'I find it ironic that Detroit is known as #motorcity and yet no one here knows how to f***ing drive'. There was a predictable backlash from local citizens, the employee was fired and Chrysler shortly afterwards ended their relationship with the agency. Clearly what had happened was that the employee tweeted thinking that he was logged into his own personal account, and not that of Chrysler. However, Chrysler did not help themselves because they removed the tweet and claimed that their account was compromised and were taking steps to resolve it, which was not well received.

However, the American Red Cross account @RedCross was also used incorrectly when an employee tweeted 'Ryan found two more 4 bottle packs of Dogfish Head's Midas Touch beer . . . when we drink we do it right #gettngslizzerd'. The Red Cross also deleted the tweet, but as they stated in their blog (www.redcrosschat.org/2011/02/16/twitter-faux-pas), 'We all know that it's impossible to really delete a tweet like this, so we acknowledged our mistake'. They apologised immediately, and also made the point that they were made up of human beings who sometimes make mistakes. While they were serious in their apology they added in a little humour and as a result many people pledged donations to them. Quick apologies and admitting errors will often go a long way to mitigating the potential negative fallout. It's always worth remembering that the internet community is made up of human beings as well, and they appreciate that everyone makes mistakes now and then.

Employees being stupid

It's really important to stress to employees that they are responsible for what they post, and if they are stupid, social media platforms have a way of bringing them to account. Two Domino's Pizza workers videoed themselves doing unmentionable things to pizzas, and a Taco Bell employee was also photographed doing disgusting things to food. Videos can go viral very quickly and the Domino's Pizza one had almost 1 million views in one day.

Both brands were badly tarnished, at least in part because they decided to try and stay 'below the radar'. Domino's decided against posting a statement on their website because they felt that would alert more of their customers to the negative story and that it 'would be like putting out a candle with a fire hose' (http://adage.com/article/news/aftermath-domino-s-pr-disaster-video/136004). What would have perhaps worked rather better would have been to try and turn the negative story into a positive one, by informing consumers that they were looking to improve their employee training process, and creating their own social media story on the way that they produced their food, and their quality control standards.

Taco Bell also hit the headlines when a video of a dozen rats running around one of their New York restaurants was uploaded to YouTube. To date this video has had over 1.6 million views. The owners apologised, but tried to downplay the incident by saying that it was a local issue in one outlet, and they also refused to discuss it further. Unfortunately social media is not local, it's global, and this particular story went around the world, with over 1000 blogs spreading the story.

It's difficult to find a positive out of such a damaging story, but it's worth making the point to employees that if something can go wrong it probably will at some point and someone will be there to video it and put it online. Rather than attempt to contain a story by trying to ignore it, it makes much more sense to have a strategy already in place to admit to failings, apologise and tell people what is going to be done to make it right.

Turning a negative into a positive

If you visit YouTube and run a search for 'Fedex delivery' or even just Fedex, if you're prepared to scroll down a screen or two, you'll find a video of an employee throwing a parcel over a fence into the garden of the addressee. This was such a shocking sight that it received 5 million views in five days (and currently has over 9 million views). Fedex quickly responded with their own reply, a video from a Senior Vice President. It was a measured reply, starting with an apology. Matthew Thornton said 'It's just not who we are. We are determined to make this right' (https://www.youtube.com/watch?v=4ESU_PcqI38). The employee was not sacked, but was instead retrained and was not working with customers. The Fedex motto was discussed, and the video was shared internally as a training aid. The VP said that they wanted to use the incident to become a better service provider in the future. I think that this is a really good example of getting a difficult situation under control quickly – admitting errors, apologising and then moving on. I don't know if they already had a policy in place for dealing with bad press of this nature, but other companies could most certainly learn from it.

Watch the news, don't just react to it

News items trend very quickly on Twitter, and are very often associated with a hashtag. Tweets should only use a hashtag if it is appropriate to do so – anything else will at best be regarded as spam and will get a hostile reaction. Even worse is when the background behind a trending hashtag isn't fully researched. In the USA there was a mass shooting at a cinema in Aurora, Colorado, and the #aurora hashtag was used in discussions. Unfortunately the @celebboutique account tweeted '#Aurora is trending, clearly about our Kim K inspired #Aurora dress ;)2'. The tweet looked in extremely poor taste and led to heavy criticism. It also didn't help that the National Rifle Association also tweeted at about the same time 'Good morning, shooters. Happy Friday! Weekend plans?' It's very easy to take a very parochial view of social media, without considering the wider world. While there isn't a problem pre-scheduling tweets, someone has to remember what is going to be tweeted when, and be in a position to do something about it in case there is any potential for negative consequences.

Another example, from Microsoft, also shows how even the big companies, who should know better, can get it catastrophically wrong. Microsoft Bing tried to use the #SupportJapan hashtag (in the days after the tsunami) as follows: 'How you can #SupportJapan – http://binged.it/fEh7iT. For every retweet, @bing will give $1 to Japan quake victims, up to $100K.' After a great deal of protest, with people viewing the tweet as Microsoft trying to take commercial advantage of a disaster, they apologised seven hours later and donated the $100,000. They also tweeted a link to their citizenship page, which explained how people could help Japan. Possibly the worst example comes from a company called Epicurious, which sent out a tweet just after the Boston Marathon bombing which said 'Boston, our hearts are with you. Here's a bowl of breakfast energy we could all use to start today'. They then compounded the problem by not responding quickly to criticism and ignoring or deleting comments on their Facebook page.

As a general rule, if something is trending, it's doing so for a reason, and it makes a great deal of sense to find out the whys and wherefores before getting involved. Don't try and jump on a bandwagon, don't try and take advantage out of a situation, and be sensitive, particularly over disasters, as people are naturally upset and may be looking for a way to vent their fear and frustration.

Don't pick a fight with the internet!

The internet is big, really big; it's bigger than any one country, any person or any company, and if you pick a fight, you are guaranteed to lose. This is something that Judith Griggs, the founder of a magazine called *Cooks Source*, didn't appreciate. She was found guilty of taking recipes posted by other people and putting them into her magazine without attribution. She then compounded this error by saying, in response to criticism '. . . the web is considered "public domain" and you should be happy we just didn't "lift" your whole article . . . the article we used written by you was in very bad need of editing, and is much better now than it was originally. We put some time into rewrites, you should compensate me.' Several parody accounts were created, online celebrities got involved, magazine advertisers were contacted and the magazine was closed down. Another company, Amy's Baking Company, was the focus of a television programme called 'Kitchen Nightmares'. The owner's actions, and negative comments on social media platforms, received a large amount of media attention, resulting in turn in negative feedback on their official Facebook page. They then took posters to task, later claiming they had been hacked and this in turn led to yet another media circus.

Trying to 'tough it out' will not work. There are far more people on the internet who are willing to take people on than can be responded to, and the more that someone tries, the more of a story it makes, and the more people get involved. The best thing to do is apologise and move on.

Summary

Those are, of course, just a few choice examples, but you have only to visit your preferred search engine and run a search for 'social media disasters' to find a rich vein of them. The one point which really comes out from all of the examples that I've given above, and the many others that are out there, is simple; respond quickly, apologise and say what you're going to do differently. That will get almost anyone out of a mess really quickly, and may well turn the situation in your favour. However, by trying to ignore it or fight back, you will only make things far worse. The best defence to any and all of these problems is to involve staff in social media, explain why it's so important and have a strong and robust social media policy.

Index

Abram, Stephen 85, 111
Alltop search engine 26
American Red Cross 161
Animoto 68, 132
Appear In 103
Ask a Librarian 103
Audacity 137
Audioboo 138
augmented reality 15, 142–3
Aurasma 143
Authorstream 27, 61
avatars 113–15
Awesome Screenshot Plus 77

BB FlashBack Express 75–6
BBC News feed 33
BBC 'Question Time' hashtag 91
BBC social media policy 153, 155, 157
BigHugeLabs 127–9
Bing 13, 163
Blackberry Messenger 4
Blackboard 81
Blogger 4, 26, 99
blogs 4, 13, 25–6, 32, 53, 99–103, 112, 125, 134
    Never seconds blog 160
    social media policy 152
    statistics 99
bookmarking 5, 27, 39–42, 69, 77, 112, 133
British Library 81, 98, 130, 139
browsers 8, 32, 39, 104

Canva 69
Carroll, Dave 8, 159–60
ccMixter 139
CD-ROM 85
chat rooms 2, 103–4
chatWING 104
Chatzy 104
Cheshire Public Library 96, 117
Chrysler Automobiles 161
cloud, the 5, 15, 39, 62, 107
Cooks Source 164
Coursera 82
Creative Commons 127, 133, 135, 139, 157
Curate Me 54
Cutts, Matt 25

Data Protection Act 2008 158
Delicious 35, 40–1, 112, 125
Digg 3
Diigo 41, 77
Domino's Pizza 161–2
Dropbox 107

Edmodo 81
e-mail 9–10
Emaze 64
embedplus 142
Essex Libraries 94–5
Essex lion 9
Everyslide 65

Facebook 2, 3, 5, 10, 11, 15, 23, 40, 47, 52, 55, 68, 93–7, 114, 122, 135
  communications tool 93–7, 99
  negative comments 96–7, 156
  social media policy 151–2, 154, 155, 157
  statistics 5, 93
  status updates 121, 122
  validity checking 12, 19–21, 25, 26–7
Fedex 162–3
Flickr 10, 25, 35, 119, 130, 134-5, 136
Flipboard 47–8
Foursquare 122–3
Futurelearn 81

Google 13, 86, 142
  Blogsearch 26, 99
  customized search engines 38–9
  Docs 107
  Drive 79
  News 125
  Ngram Viewer 3
  properties 23–5
Google+ 4, 11, 13, 23, 24, 27, 48, 52, 119, 122, 125
  communities 98
  Hangouts 65, 78–80
  +1 24, 120

Haikudeck 68
hashtags 11, 21, 48, 65, 91–3, 96, 124, 150, 151, 163
Haverhill Public Library 154
HiddenEloise 9
Hoax-Slayer 20
home pages 32–6
Hootsuite 92–3, 124

images 11, 18, 27, 34, 36, 53, 64, 68, 69, 76–7, 81, 99, 102, 105, 112–3, 119, 122, 127–33, 135, 136, 140
infographics 136–7
Instagram 135
Internet Archive 138

Keep Calm posters 129
Kindle 6
'Kitchen Nightmares' 164
Klout 21–2, 120, 124

Knovio 60–1

Learnist 53
Library of Congress 130, 135, 139
Library Success wiki 104
LinkedIn 2, 3, 5, 10, 27, 117, 97–8, 118, 119, 140
  validity checking 23
LIS Wiki 104
LiveJournal 4

Magisto 141
makerspaces 121
Mention 124–5
Meograph 66–7
Microsoft Office 59, 61–2, 107
MOOCs 81–2
Mozilla Popcorn Maker 142
MyJugaad 69
MyPicPals 68, 132
MySpace 2, 3

National Library of Australia 149
National Trust 11
Netvibes 35–6, 125
Never seconds blog 160–1

Padlet 106
Paper.li 51–3
Participoll 62
Pearltrees 36–8
Picmonkey 131
Pinterest 11, 27, 99, 103, 112, 119, 122, 130, 133–4, 135, 136, 140, 158
Pixiclip 81
Podbean 138
podcasting 137–40
Podomatic 138
Potter, Ned 63–4
PowerPoint 59–62, 63, 64, 68, 70
Powtoon 69–70
Presentain 61
Prezi 62–4
Projeqt 65
Pulp-o-mizer 129

Qualman, Erik 119
Quozio 129

Return on Investment (ROI) 119–20
RSS 14, 31, 33, 36, 42, 52, 69, 125

Scoop.it! 11, 49–51
screencapture 76–8
screencasting 73–6
Screencast-o-matic 74
Screenr 74
search engine optimization (SEO) 27,
    121–2
Seattle Public Library 139
Silobreaker search engine 26
slides 65
Slideshare.net 27, 65, 78
Smore 129
SnapCrab 77
Snipping tool 76–7
Snopes 20
social media
    criticism 150
    definition 4, 149
    misunderstandings 115–6
    policy 116, 147–58
    statistics 5, 87, 99, 133, 134
SocialMention* search engine 21, 88,
    125
Soundbible 138
Soundcloud 138
South Holland Library 153
spreaker 138
start pages see home pages
StatusPeople Fake Followers 22
sticky notes 105–6
Storify 65
Sullivan, Danny 23–4
Swayy 53–4
Symbaloo 32–4
Szoter 77–8

tablet-based applications 33, 47–8, 52,
    60, 104, 121, 135, 141, 143
Taco Bell 161–2
Tagxedo 131
Talkwalker Alerts 125
Technorati search engine 26
Timeglider 67

timelines 66–7
TinyTake 77
Topeka and Shawnee County Public
    Library 122–3
Topsy search engine 21, 92, 125
Tweetbeep 125
Tweetdeck 47, 93
Tweeted Times 47
Tweriod 91
twibbons 114
Twitter 5, 7, 9, 10, 11, 52, 65, 111, 114,
    119, 149, 154
    as a communication tool 87–93
    avatar 113
    hashtags 91–2
    lists 46–47, 90
    search engine 92
    social media disasters 161
    social media policy 150–1
    statistics 5, 13, 87, 155
    validity checking 18, 21–2, 26
Tyler, Alyson 51
Typepad 26

United Airlines 159–60

Vine 140–1

weblog see blog
websites 12, 86–7
    ranking with search engines 27
    spoofs 17
Wefollow search engine 21, 88
wiki 4, 104–5
WikiMatrix 105
Wikipedia 131 142 153
WizIQ 80
word clouds 130–1
WordPress 26

YouTube 4, 8, 24, 28, 138, 140
    editing videos 142
    statistics 13 93

Zite 47–8